Self-Publishing on Amazon 2017

No publisher? No Agent? No Problem!

By Dr. Andy Williams

ezSEONews.com

GW00802452

Version 1.0

Published on 4th July 2017

DISCLAIMER AND TERMS OF USE AGREEMENT

The author and publisher of this eBook and the accompanying materials have used their best efforts in preparing this eBook. The author and publisher make no representation or warranties with respect to the accuracy, applicability, fitness, or completeness of the contents of this eBook. The information contained in this eBook is strictly for educational purposes. Therefore, if you wish to apply ideas contained in this eBook, you are taking full responsibility for your actions.

The author and publisher disclaim any warranties (express or implied), merchantability, or fitness for any particular purpose. The author and publisher shall in no event be held liable to any party for any direct, indirect, punitive, special, incidental or other consequential damages arising directly or indirectly from any use of this material, which is provided "as is", and without warranties.

The author and publisher do not warrant the performance, effectiveness or applicability of any sites listed or linked to in this eBook.

All links are for information purposes only and are not warranted for content, accuracy or any other implied or explicit purpose.

The author and publisher of this book are not in any way associated with Google.

Contents

Opportunity knocks 1

    Growth of eBooks and eReaders over traditional print books 1

    But aren't eBooks Dead? 3

    References 4

Successful self-published authors 5

    J. A. Konrath 5

    John Locke 6

    Amanda Hocking 7

    E. L. James 8

My own Kindle success 10

    But success isn't guaranteed 10

Using Amazon for research 11

    Amazon's auto-complete search box 11

    Competitor research 15

    Making sense of the sales rank 20

    Potential profits from book sales 21

Writing & formatting your book 23

Creating a style for your books 24

    Which Font? 25

    Quick Style Buttons 26

    Quickly changing the default font for your style 28

The Essential Sections of your Book 35

    Before the Main Book Content 35

    After the Main Book Content 35

Important formatting rules 36

    Headings 36

    Paragraphs, carriage returns, and page breaks 38

Page breaks 39

Hyperlinks 40

Lists.. 41

Images.. 41

    Image size 41

    How to insert an image................................... 45

    Color images v black & white 46

Page numbers.. 47

    Page Numbering in Word................................... 47

    Step-by-step instructions 47

    Table of contents 50

        Updating a TOC 52

    Previewing your book....................................... 53

        Saving as Web Page, Filtered........................ 54

    If you are happy, zip it up. 58

    What about Google Docs?................................. 60

Editor v DIY Proofing 62

Kindle book covers.. 64

    Where to get "professional" covers done for you? 65

        The cheapest option 65

    A little more expensive 66

    Higher priced covers....................................... 66

Publishing on Amazon 68

    Uploading your book to Amazon 68

    The book title... 70

    Is your book part of a series?........................... 71

    The book edition number 71

    Author.. 71

A note about pen names 72

Contributors...72

The book description 73

Publishing rights...74

Keywords 74

Categories 75

Age and Grade Range...78

Pre-Order 78

Kindle eBook Preview...80

Kindle eBook ISBN 82

KDP Select Enrollment 83

Territories 83

Rights & pricing..83

Choose your royalty rate 84

Thoughts on pricing 85

Matchbook 86

Book Lending 86

Updating your book 87

Promoting your new Kindle book... 89

Setting up a Gmail account..91

Already own a Gmail account? 91

Your first Gmail account? 92

Step 1 - High-quality book & cover..92

Step 2 - Facebook page 93

Setting up a Facebook page 93

Facebook & Pennames...94

Step 3 - Twitter account 98

Setting up a Twitter account for your author name.....................99

If you set up a blog...101

Step 4 – Author Central..102

Author page URL...108

Adding new books to your author profile..110

Step 5 – Get downloads, reviews & likes on Amazon...................................111

Setting up the Free Promotion in Amazon 113

Free promotion schedule..114

Lists of sites that can promote your book...115

Kindle Countdown Deals 116

Step 6 - The "Look Inside" feature...116

A note for fiction writers..118

Step 7 - Serialization of your books...119

What not to do when promoting your book...121

How Facebook page & Twitter fit into your promotional strategy....................122

Using YouTube to promote your books 122

Setting up tracking links 122

Tracking sales of your book 126

Other eBook platforms..128

Non-US publishers...129

Where to go from here..130

Create the paperback 130

Publishing as a Paperback 131

How big will your book be?..132

Price calculator...132

Converting to Createspace Format 138

Check #1 – Page Size & Margins...138

Check #2 – Correct use of styles..138

Check # 2 – Links 139

Check #3 - Numbered Lists 139

Check #4 - Layout 139

    Problem 1 - Empty lines at the top of a page 140

    Problem 2 - Headers at the bottom of pages 140

Check #5 - TOC update & check 142

Check #6 - Page numbers start on right-hand side 142

Check #7 - Image DPI "requirements" 143

Images in Word 144

Adding a new title to Createspace 146

Downloading a Cover Template 158

Understanding the book cover templates 160

    Areas marked on the templates 160

    The Spine 162

Submitting the book cover to Createspace 166

    Expanded Distribution? 169

Feedback from Createspace, and the next step 175

    Please leave a review/thought on Amazon 178

Useful resources 179

    Publishing Tutorials 179

    My ezSEONews Website 179

    My other Webmaster books 179

    My Video Courses 179

Appendix I 180

    HTML coding 180

    A Note on HTML formatting 183

What People are Saying about previous versions of this book & Andy Williams

"Authors was very good in explaining the whole process with tons of details. I had read many ebooks in regards of Kindle Publishing, this is by far the best one". **Fred C**

"I'm reading so many Kindle publishing and formatting books these days to figure out this beast and this is one of the best. Clear, well organized, well written". **Helen C. Page**

"I liked the most that the author is giving at the very beginning the examples of authors who did exceptionally well with Kindle publishing and then shows his own figures. That for me is great because it is motivating and I like people who write from their own experience". **Francesca**

"Dr. Andy Williams is someone I have been reading for several years, on a wide variety of Internet-related topics, and I have found him to be knowledgeable and ethical". **Rosana Hart**

"I was actually in the process of publishing a Kindle book when I opened this and I have to say it's filled out my knowledge in this area better than anything else I have seen or read. It's so complete you may not use it all the very first time you publish, but I think you can go back to it again for more detail as you get more deeply into the process, or publish a second book. Everything is laid out in a step by step way with illustrations". **Inisheer**

"Thank you for this book, Dr. Andy! It is very comprehensive and I discovered new information that I was previously unaware of. I definitely recommend this book for all Kindle Publishers - it has many great tips and wise advice". **Kerry**

*"Andy covers just about every question I had in my mind, as well as quite a few that I hadn't thought of. He does so in an easy to read, relaxed style that demystifies the Kindle publishing process". **Martin Avis***

*"What I like about this book is that there are no dirty tricks that could get you in trouble. An easy ABC read for even my 13-year-old who will be writing her own book during half-term". **C. Mulenga***

*"Another of Andy's well thought out and executed products. Everything you need to know about publishing and promoting your new book on the Kindle". **Minichester***

*"Although I've already published several books on Kindle, there were plenty of great ideas here that I could take away and use. Love the stories at the beginning, followed by practical how-to steps, for each section". **SalisburyOne***

*"I've read a lot of info on Kindle publishing and found that this book covers everything from a to z. It's inspired me to have another go as I can see where I went wrong on my first attempt. Time well invested in reading it IMHO". **Vicky Bellamy***

*"Like many, I have read several books on Kindle publishing. Some go into mind-numbing detail, others are light weight. Andy has got the balance absolutely right for newbie (Kindle) authors. An excellent read with great content and several web links to useful resources". **Keith Finney***

A Note About UK v US English

There are some differences between UK and US English. While I try to be consistent, some errors may slip into my writing because I spend a lot of time corresponding to people in both the UK and the US. The line can blur.

Examples of this include spelling of words like optimise (UK) v optimize (US).

The difference I get the most complaints about is with collective nouns. Collective nouns refer to a group of individuals, e.g. Google. In the US, collective nouns are singular, so **Google IS** a search engine. However, in the UK, collective nouns are usually plural, so **Google ARE** a search engine.

There are other differences too. I hope that if I have been inconsistent somewhere in this book, it does not detract from the value you get from it.

Found Typos in this book?

Errors can get through proofreaders, so if you do find any typos or grammatical errors in this book, I'd be very grateful if you could let me know using this email address:

typos@ezseonews.com

URLs in this book

Ideally, I would love it if everyone could click a URL to be taken to a web page referenced in this book. However, I realize that paperback books don't offer such a luxury. Whenever I linked to a web page with a long URL, I used a shortened version of the URL to make it easier to type in. For trust and safety, I chose to use the link shortener owned by Google (https://goo.gl/).

Opportunity knocks

I would never have attempted to publish my own books at any other time in our history.

That's a bold statement...

The thing is, the Kindle revolution has made it so easy that if you aspire to be a published author, now IS the time. Today, you don't have to send out hundreds of letters to publishers or agents. You don't have to receive hundreds of rejection letters back. Even if you do get a literary agent interested in your work, there are so many people involved in the decision to publish your book that there's no guarantee you'll get it in print. That's not even mentioning how your profits will be eaten away by the various people involved in the process. Each will take their cut.

Today, you can write a book and self-publish it on Amazon for FREE and ANYONE can do it. Not only that, but you can earn up to 70% royalties on your book sales! We are at a special time in history where opportunity really is knocking. The tides are turning against traditional print books in favor of "eBooks" and this is giving independent (indie) authors the upper hand.

Let's have a look at some of the facts.

Growth of eBooks and eReaders over traditional print books

The phenomenon of eBooks and eReaders has brought about revolutionary changes in the book publishing industry. Ebooks and eReaders suit the needs of the modern man who requires permanent access to his library no matter where he is in the world.

In the technology era, where electronic devices have become indispensable in both professional and private life, reading habits have changed accordingly. At the same time, people have become more mobile; they commute longer distances, change their workplace more frequently, and travel more often to far away destinations. As a consequence, private libraries have become mobile with the introduction of eBooks and eReaders. In order to create a digital library, a reader needs either an eReader (such as Kindle or Nook) or a tablet (iPad, Kindle Fire, Android tablet or even a Samsung Galaxy Note "Phablet").

You can even use your Smartphone as an eReader, although the text may be a little small for long periods of reading and any graphics difficult to make out. The greatest feature of many eReaders is their excellent readability thanks to electronic paper technology. Tablets, on the other hand, are popular due to the fact that they can be used for a multitude of purposes. Tablet users browse the internet, watch videos, read books, and shop online with their electronic devices.

There are a number of different reasons why the sale of eBooks, eReaders, and tablets is booming. For a start, eBooks are greener, cheaper, and more convenient. Electronic publishing reduces the consumption of natural resources and the level of pollution too, because it does not incur the costs that traditional printing does. As a result, the price of eBooks is considerably lower than that of traditional paper books.

Instead of piling up physical books at home, readers build up a virtual library that is light, transportable, and easily manageable. An eBook comes with additional features, such as text search, highlights, bookmarks, and notes. What's more, an eBook instantly available and is just a click away thanks to online shopping.

Browsing the online bookstores and finding the right book has proven to be a much more efficient way to shop for an average reader. And the ever-growing number of available digital books provides a broad range of titles. Books in certain niches, and specialty books, are so much easier to find on the internet than in the high street, and the buyer can purchase worldwide.

The flourishing market for eBooks and eReaders has opened up a whole new world for authors. Most of all, writers have welcomed the possibility of self-publishing their work in the form of electronic books. Self-publishing represents a challenging alternative to traditional publishing in the sense that it gives the writer more freedom, flexibility, and visibility. Higher revenues, sole copyrights, freedom of choice (regarding format and design), quick access to the marketplace, and direct contact with the readers, are just some of the appealing aspects of self-publishing as opposed to traditional publishing. So, how does the growing trend of eBooks and eReaders help all those who would like to venture into digital self-publishing?

First of all, authors have the option to bridge the gap between themselves and the readers by publishing their books online without the use of publishers as intermediaries. Instead, authors can reach the global marketplace fairly quickly and effectively by using one of the publishing platforms, such as Amazon's Kindle, Barnes and Noble's NookPress, Apple's iBookstore, or Google Book. All of these platforms are free to use. Authors just sign up, upload their eBook, and receive royalties from the platform, varying between 40% and 80%. Some of these platforms will even auto-convert uploaded eBooks into their own format and paperback.

Following this self-publishing route, authors no longer need to find a publisher to accept their book. Now, they simply upload their work to the different platforms and within hours, their book is available for sale. If they are very successful, they still have the option to publish a hardback or a paperback edition with a publishing company (this is the route taken by E. L. James with her 50 Shades trilogy). Furthermore, editors, proofreaders, and graphic designers, necessary for a traditional book, are not essential when self-publishing. Depending on the budget and the topic, authors can search the internet for available services or do most of the formatting and design work themselves. In contrast to traditional publishing, self-published authors retain their copyrights and thereby considerably increase their own revenues once their eBooks are sold.

A huge success story in the self-publishing world is Smashwords. Founded in 2008, Smashwords is the "world's largest distributor of indie ebooks", and "..make it fast and free for anyone, anywhere in the world, to publish and distribute ebooks to major retailers and thousands of libraries"[1].

At Smashwords, authors can get 85% (or more) of the net revenues from the sale of their books, and they still retain all the rights. Contrary to the earlier prejudices against self-publishers, the latest developments with platforms such as Smashwords, prove that self-published books are gaining more and more visibility. Library Direct is the project launched by Smashwords for big libraries and databases to gain access to books published on Smashwords.

Authors who turn to self-publishing will need to carefully structure their marketing plan. Since there's no big publishing company in charge of publicity, the writers themselves must use all of the available channels of communication to promote the sale of their books. This can include social media like Facebook and Twitter (though in truth, this often becomes more important as you "grow" as an author). Many "indie" writers set up a website or blog which can be used to promote their books and communicate with their audience.

The boom in e-publishing not only represents a great advantage for those in need of a mobile and easily accessible library, but also a massive opportunity for those who want to publish their own work.

But aren't eBooks Dead?

It's true that eBook sales have been on the decline in recent months, as younger generations yearn for that paperback experience. However, to say eBooks are dead is vastly incorrect. A more appropriate term might be that sales have plateaued. According to the Guardian newspaper, in 2016, eBooks had a 25% share in book sales, compared to 26% in 2015, but only 18% in 2012[2] (when I first started publishing my own books on Amazon).

While digital eBooks will continue to offer self-published authors a great opportunity, I recommend you publish in both digital and paperback versions because there isn't a lot of extra work to do this. This book has you covered. In it, I will show you how to publish both digital and paperback versions so your books are available in both formats on the biggest online bookstore in the world - Amazon.

Before we look at the mechanics of self-publishing, I want to talk a little about some success stories.

References

1.   https://www.smashwords.com/about

2.   https://goo.gl/ukaNbd

Successful self-published authors

J. A. Konrath

You can find his website here:

http://www.jakonrath.com/

.. and his blog here:

http://jakonrath.blogspot.com

J. A. Konrath's blog is a mine of information. Every year in December he updates what he calls *"Konrath's resolutions for writers"* which serves as a testimony of how much the book industry has changed since 2006, notably with the advent of e-books. It does the author great credit to not have erased a single entry on the list, and to include sentences such as this: *"I've lived long enough to see my advice become obsolete, and that gives me hope for the future"*. Not surprisingly, Konrath has embraced the new possibilities that e-books offer, such as the opportunity to self-publish on Amazon, and not grieving the loss of an old world, but welcoming change.

The man behind the blog is a writer with a good heart, who believes in a community of writers lending each other a hand. He teaches writing at Dupage College, Illinois, and has written fiction under the pen names Jack Kilborn, Joe Kimball, and of course, his own name J. A. Konrath. He likes to write horror (usually under the pen name Jack Kilborn), with titles like *Afraid* and *Trapped*. The series of novels popularly known as the *"Jack Daniels"* series (including *Whiskey Sour* or *Rusty Nail)* are some of his top sellers. He describes his own work as *"A cross between the scares of Thomas Harris and the laughs of Dave Barry"*.

After reading about him and the way he struggled through the endless rejections of his first nine novels, many writers would have felt depressed and defeated. However, J.A. Konrath's message to aspiring writers is that it is very possible to make a living as a genre fiction writer. His optimism is backed by useful tips on how to self-publish in a more effective way.

Spend some time on his blog and read his tips and motivational pieces. After reading his blog, you should be left with one overwhelming message. If you are not enjoying success, you cannot blame anyone but yourself. Write a good book, turn it into an e-book, and make it available online. Oh, and make sure you do it NOW!

John Locke

Some stories are worth reading because they take you, the reader, into a sequence of action and suspense scenes where you don't know what is going to happen next. It might be late at night and you might have to get up early for work the next day, but your mind craves another page, or perhaps just another paragraph – but you need to know what happens next. This quality is what John Locke describes as "punch". He wants his stories to have "punch" and most of his readers agree that they do.

John Locke is the best-selling author of some 17 novels and a book of non-fiction about how to sell e-books. His best-known works are the *Donovan Creed* novels. Starting with *Lethal People,* Mr. Locke introduces Donovan Creed, an ex-CIA agent who works for an obscure agency. Despite seeming like a classic "tough guy" and being a ruthless murderer when necessary, Donovan has a heart and a way with women. He has of course written other books, like *Emmet & Gentry*, or *Bad Doctor* - and created some other well-crafted characters like *Emmet Love* or *Dani Ripper*. This combination of "punch" and appealing characters is Mr. Locke's formula for producing one page-turner after another. In 2011 alone he wrote nine books.

John Locke's story is an interesting one.

He began writing fiction as a way to relax after having open-heart surgery. He enjoyed it so much that he decided to try self-publishing his work in print. This was at a great personal cost and with little success. Then, in March 2010, he decided to e-publish the same three novels and sell each book for only 99 cents on Amazon. By 2011, his sales had reached huge figures and one of his novels, *Saving Rachel,* had even reached number 1 on Amazon. His promotional strategy was simple. An attractive cover and product description, a well-edited final product, and effective self-promotion on social networks like Facebook and Twitter.

You can read John Locke's blog here:

https://johnlockeauthor.wordpress.com/

You'll notice that John doesn't post very often to his blog. His strategy is to write a blog post that will resonate with his target audience, and then draw them to the blog post via social channels like Twitter. If you are part of his target audience, chances are that his blog posts will resonate with you. They'll bring out emotions as you read them and this is what he wants. He wants that connection with his readers. It's much easier to sell to someone when you have that connection. John's strategy is all about building those relationships, and it doesn't matter what business you are in, it's a smart way to go if you can pull it off.

Amanda Hocking

You can read Amanda Hocking's story on her website:

http://worldofamandahocking.com/

Her life story tells of a penniless young lady living in Austin, Minnesota, and how she spent late nights writing book after book in an effort to be published by the end of 2009. Like many aspiring authors, her efforts resulted in a lot of rejection letters from various publishing houses. In 2010, Amanda found out about Elisa Lorello and her novel entitled 'Faking It'. That book had made it into the top 100 on Kindle, and Elisa did it without a publisher. Things quickly started falling into place as Amanda discovered other successful self-published authors (including J.A. Konrath).

Although still not totally convinced about self-publishing, Amanda decided to give it a go. There was a Jim Henson exhibit coming to Chicago later in the year and she wanted to go. She decided to try self-publishing in an effort to make enough money to cover the costs of attending the Muppet exhibition. All she needed was a couple of hundred bucks.

The rest is history really. Amanda made the "couple hundred bucks" to go to the exhibit. In fact, she made a lot more.

In June 2010 she made $3180.

In July 2010 she made $6527.

In August 2010, she was on track to make $9000 - $10,000.

Compare this to her previous year's income. In 2009, working her day job, Amanda grossed $18,000.

If you check Amanda's Wikipedia entry, you'll get a few more stats on her. Here is an amazing stat that will surely inspire you:

By March 2011, she had sold over a million copies of her nine books and earned two million dollars from the sales. In early 2011, she was averaging 9,000 book sales a day!

Amanda's massive success was down to her decision to take the self-publishing route!

Amanda Hocking has become a prophet of change in the book world, despite her own reluctance to accept such an honor. In spite of the popularity her work has earned her, it is safe to say she will not be remembered so much for it, as for the implications her success has had for the very foundations of the publishing industry. Her example is already being followed by thousands of other writers, tired of facing constant setbacks and rejection from publishing houses.

In March 2011, Miss Hocking signed a contract with St. Martin's Press for 4 of her books. It was a deal worth 2 million US dollars. Would she ever have signed a contract like this if she had not already become hugely successful as a self-published author?

E. L. James

E. L. James is Erika Leonard's pen name, under which this British housewife wrote the best-selling *Fifty Shades* trilogy. She initially e-published her novels, but after the huge success they enjoyed in that format, she signed a deal with Vintage Books to publish all three titles. Their popularity soared to the point that they surpassed the previous UK book sales record of 4 million, reaching 5.3 million with the first book in the trilogy, *Fifty Shades of Grey*. Her global sales are just as spectacular. E.L. James has sold more than 40 million copies (and rising) of her novels worldwide, not to mention film and TV deals.

On her website, she assures her readers that no one has been more surprised by her success than herself. She wants to come across as a very normal person. E.L. James is a married, middle-aged woman, and mother of two, living in the leafy suburbs of London.

She got the inspiration for her trilogy from Stephenie Meyer's trilogy *Twilight*, though her 50 Shades is a much steamier read.

Erika's success started when she reportedly posted the story in a *Twilight* fan fiction forum. It was word-of-mouth that fueled the spread of her book. Her success story shows once again how a completely normal person, with no initial advantages other than imagination (and a little patience and dedication), can achieve phenomenal success.

You can read E.L. James blog here:

http://www.eljamesauthor.com/

J.A. Konrath, John Locke, Amanda Hocking and E.L. James are 4 big hitters in the self-publishing world, but there are many, many more successful people like this. These writers show that it is possible for ordinary people, with determination and drive, to succeed as self-published authors. Sure, J. A. Konrath teaches writing, but that does not mean you have to be a great writer to enjoy success. Telling a good story is enough.

These 4 were among those that inspired me to give it a go. I am only just starting on my journey, but since you bought my book, it's only fair that I tell you about my success so far.

My own Kindle success

I published my first book on the Kindle platform in August 2012. By December 2012 (5 months after starting), I was already making what many people would consider a full-time income from my Kindle books. Oh, and I was only working part-time.

Here is the data:

August 2012 - $6.27

September 2012 - $278.09

October 2012 - $1492.66

November 2012 - $1958.73

December 2012 - $2989.18

That's from zero to nearly $3000 a month in 5 months working part-time. That income was mainly from 3 books. I had 4 books at the time. Today I have over 20 in both Kindle and paperback versions.

But success isn't guaranteed

This sounds like a strange thing to be telling you before you even start self-publishing, but it's true. I make good money from my self-published books, but it was a lot of work, experimentation, sweat, and tears. One thing I have learned is that having a great book is not enough. I have a few books that I think are great but they don't sell, at all. I have other books that I think are great that do. So, what is the difference?

The most important thing that will make your book sell, or not, is whether there is a pre-existing audience for it. You can write the best, most authoritative and entertaining book on the mating habits of earthworms, but if nobody is interested, it won't sell.

No one wants to invest weeks of work into a book that flops. To be brutally honest, there is no sure-fire way of knowing whether a book will sell or not, but, there are some very good indicators we can look at, and this is where we'll start our journey, by using Amazon as a research tool.

Using Amazon for research

Amazon provides us with a lot of useful information about our intended genre or niche. We can use it to learn about the competition we face and whether or not there is an audience for our intended work. Using Amazon, we can find out if a particular book is selling and roughly estimate how many sales it makes each day. This can be useful information for authors because we can see whether a book we want to write is likely to have an audience. Think about it. If you knew that books in your chosen niche weren't selling, would you still write the book?

Similarly, if you were looking for a topic to write about, then seeing books selling very well in a particular niche would be interesting. We'll look at the kind of information we can get on 'any book' on Amazon shortly. First, I want to show you a cool way to brainstorm book ideas.

Amazon's auto-complete search box

Amazon's search box tries to complete what you type. If I go over there and start to type in the word "zombies", look what happens:

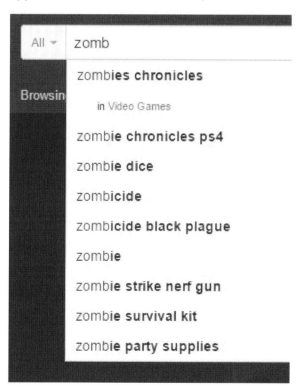

Amazon lists the phrases that it thinks I might be interested in.

Where does it get these phrases from?

Well, Amazon isn't telling, but I'd bet it was based on search queries that previous visitors had typed in, with the most commonly typed search phrases at the top!

This can be a great tool for niche research, especially if we narrow our search to the books department. After all, we are only really interested in the books that Amazon customers are searching for. You can see these suggestions are different from those we received when searching all departments earlier.

And you'll get slightly different suggestions if you search in the Kindle section of Amazon:

I can see right there that my idea for a zombie apocalypse book would probably have an audience!

Looking at the order of the phrases, it makes sense that these would be in the order of search volume. I mean "zombie" would be the most commonly searched for word in this niche, wouldn't it? Every search phrase that someone would type into Amazon when looking for a book on zombies, would include that word. Therefore, we can see which of the phrases are more popular. That's a great start for our niche/genre research.

One thing to bear in mind is that the auto-complete suggestions you are seeing are the same auto-complete suggestions other visitors will see.

Why is that useful to remember?

Well, when you are looking for "search keywords" for your book (see later), then choosing phrases which appear in these lists is a smart way to go. Think about it for a minute. A lot of people will end up clicking on one of the auto-complete suggestions, meaning they end up searching for that term. If your book is ranking for that search term, then you've just delivered eyeballs to your book cover. By using phrases from this auto-complete feature, you don't have to second guess what people are searching for. You just need to take Amazon's suggestions and make sure you rank for those phrases.

You can actually extract a huge amount of information from an auto-complete search tool by structuring your search.

Look what happens when I type the letter "a" after the word "zombie":

Amazon tries to complete the phrase even though I've only typed an "a". What we end up with is a lot of phrases that people are searching for starting with "zombie a". What if you repeated this search with "zombie b"?

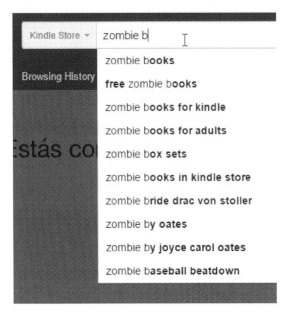

Go on. Try "zombie c" and "zombie d".

You can go through the entire alphabet to find some really great book ideas.

Here's one that actually made me feel a little queasy:

Zombie love? A zombie love story?

How would that work? A zombie in love with a zombie? A zombie in love with a human? Surely not a human in love with a zombie?

I suppose whatever floats your boat! There are loads of small niches within larger genres and if you find one with a rabid audience (pun intended), so much the better.

Besides getting great ideas for books, these auto-complete search phrases are excellent keywords to keep for later. When you submit your book, you'll need to enter suggested "search keywords". Therefore, keep a list of relevant search terms for later reference.

We can also determine whether there is an existing audience for our books, by spying on our would-be competitors.

Let's use Amazon for that...

Competitor research

In the search box at the top, select **Kindle Store** and enter the phrase you want to research:

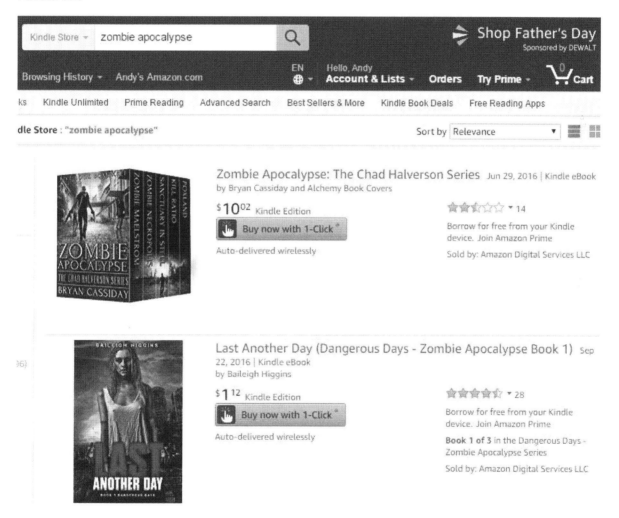

Amazon will show you your competition as a set of search results. You can quickly check the price on competing books and see if these books are getting many reviews. However, the real research begins when we click through to one of the book's product pages.

Last Another Day (Dangerous Days - Zombie Apocalypse Book 1) Kindle Edition

by Baileigh Higgins ▾ (Author)

★★★★☆ ▾   28 customer reviews

Book 1 of 3 in Dangerous Days (3 Book Series)

▸ See all formats and editions

Kindle
$1.12

Read with Our **Free App**

The Dead Rise

Trapped in the shower by the monster that was once her husband, Morgan's survival hinges on her willingness to kill the man she loves.

Realizing that his family needs him, Max takes a risk and runs

▾ Read more

READ ON
ANY DEVICE
› Get free Kindle app

I can quickly see that this particular book is part of a series. It's book one of three. I can also see that this book is only available as a Kindle book. There is no paperback version. I can tell this because if a paperback version existed, it would be listed in the formats section, like this:

▸ See all 2 formats and editions

Kindle
$3.81

Read with Our **Free App**

Paperback
$11.69

4 Used from $12.70
12 New from $11.68

The book description is worth reading, as it will give you an idea of what is selling in this niche (assuming this book does sell and we'll discover that in a moment). You might also pick up on some words or phrases being used that you can add to your list of relevant keywords.

Under the product description section is a really useful section called "Customers who bought this item also bought".

Customers who bought this item also bought Page 1 of 20

    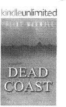

Die Another Day (Dangerous Days - Zombie Apocalypse Book 3)
› Baileigh Higgins
⭐⭐⭐⭐⭐ 1
Kindle Edition
$3.00

Survive Another Day (Dangerous Days - Zombie Apocalypse Book 2)
› Baileigh Higgins
⭐⭐⭐⭐☆ 1
Kindle Edition
$1.12

Dead Haven: A Zombie Novel (Jack Zombie Book 1)
› Flint Maxwell
⭐⭐⭐⭐☆ 33
Kindle Edition
$1.12

Outbreak (The Brother's Creed Book 1)
› Joshua C. Chadd
⭐⭐⭐⭐½ 84
Kindle Edition
$1.12

Dead Coast: A Zombie Novel (Jack Zombie Book 4)
› Flint Maxwell
⭐⭐⭐⭐⭐ 6
Kindle Edition
$4.03

This is great information to have. I now know that people who bought this zombie book, also buy other zombie books. See "Page 1 of 20" in the top right of the screenshot? That means customers who bought this one book, also tended to buy one of around 100 other zombie books (assuming 5 suggestions per page). That's a good indicator that the zombie niche is a profitable one. Compare that to a book on chocolate cakes:

Customers who bought this item also bought

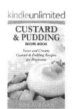 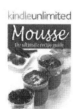  

Custard and Pudding Recipe Book: Sweet and Creamy Custard and...
Les Ilagan
⭐⭐⭐⭐⭐ 1
Kindle Edition
$3.89

Mousse – The Ultimate Recipe Guide
Terri Smitheen
⭐⭐⭐⭐½ 14
Kindle Edition
$3.34

Secrets of a Jewish Baker: Recipes for 125 Breads from Around the World
› George Greenstein
⭐⭐⭐⭐½ 106
Kindle Edition
$24.81

Cakes: 150 Best Cake Recipes Of All Time (Baking Cookbooks,...
› Paula Isabella
⭐⭐☆☆☆ 5
Kindle Edition
$4.27

Only 4 books in the "also bought" section.

Scroll down to the **Product Details** section of the page:

Product details

File Size: 3531 KB
Print Length: 274 pages
Simultaneous Device Usage: Unlimited
Publication Date: September 22, 2016
Sold by: Amazon Digital Services LLC
Language: English
ASIN: B01LZKV7BI
Text-to-Speech: Enabled ☑
X-Ray: Not Enabled ☑
Word Wise: Enabled
Lending: Not Enabled
Screen Reader: Supported ☑
Enhanced Typesetting: Enabled ☑
Amazon Best Sellers Rank: #3,386 Paid in Kindle Store (See Top 100 Paid in Kindle Store)
   #19 in Books > Literature & Fiction > Genre Fiction > Horror > **Occult**
   #20 in Kindle Store > Kindle eBooks > Literature & Fiction > Horror > **Occult**
   #45 in Books > Science Fiction & Fantasy > Science Fiction > **Genetic Engineering**

The file size at the top doesn't tell us how long the book is. It could be a very short book with lots of photos! However, Amazon does show an estimated print length, so we get an idea of how many pages the book has. That's much more useful information because we can then tell whether the books that are selling are long or short.

For example, if I wanted to write a comprehensive book on baking, but saw that all of the baking books that sold well were actually quite short, then that would suggest I might be better off splitting my book into smaller, niche baking guides.

The page length coupled with the cost of the book can also help guide us when we come to price our own publication.

At the bottom of the **Product Details** is the **Amazon Best Sellers Rank**. This one ranks 3,386 in paid Kindle. That means there are only 3,385 books on Kindle that sell more than this one. Is that good? Well, we'll see in a moment. For now, just remember that the lower the Amazon Best Sellers Rank number is, the more that book sells.

When you are researching competing books, you might see that the Amazon Best Sellers Rank looks a little different.

Product Details

File Size: 111 KB

Print Length: 21 pages

Sold by: Amazon Digital Services, Inc.

Language: English

ASIN: B0060QEAEU

Text-to-Speech: Enabled ☑

X-Ray: Not Enabled ☑

Lending: Not Enabled

Amazon Best Sellers Rank: #4,778 Free in Kindle Store

This book is ranked **4,778 Free in Kindle Store**.

As we'll see later, you can give your book away for free and this one is clearly doing that at the moment. Amazon ranks free books in a separate chart. This one ranks 4,778 in that chart, so only 4,777 free books are downloaded more often than this one.

It is easier to rank in the free charts than the paid section, so you can largely ignore any seller ranks in the free Kindle store. They do not give you an idea of potential sales.

At the very bottom of the product detail section, you'll see the categories where the current book ranks.

Amazon Best Sellers Rank: #3,386 Paid in Kindle Store (See Top 100 Paid in Kindle Store)
  #19 in Books > Literature & Fiction > Genre Fiction > Horror > **Occult**
  #20 in Kindle Store > Kindle eBooks > Literature & Fiction > Horror > **Occult**
  #45 in Books > Science Fiction & Fantasy > Science Fiction > **Genetic Engineering**

These categories can give you an idea of categories for your own book, but there is a problem. When you come to submit your book, the categories available are not the same ones you see in these product detail listings. We'll come back to that later.

The customer reviews are also really useful for research. Reviews offer feedback from people that read the book. Spend time going through the reviews of competing books and making notes on what people liked, what they disliked, and what they wished the book had included. When you write your book, you can make sure you don't make the same mistakes as these other authors. At the same time, you can include any good ideas.

Have a look to see what other information is available on each of your competitor's product pages. The information changes frequently, but I have covered the main areas that I look at when researching a book. Now, let's find out what the Amazon Best Sellers Rank really means in terms of sales.

Making sense of the sales rank

The first thing to know is that the Best Sellers Rank (BSR) is calculated independently at each of the Amazon stores.

Remember BSR is the rank order of how books sell. A BSR of 1 means it's the top-selling book on Amazon. A BSR of 10,000 means it's the 10,000th best-selling book on Amazon.

Also bear in mind that the #1 bestseller on Amazon.co.uk will sell a lot less than the #1 bestseller on Amazon.com, even though they have the same BSR.

The figures I am going to give here refer to the Amazon.com only. If you want to estimate book sales from Best Seller Rank, go to Amazon.com to check out the ranks there.

Amazon doesn't tell us how BSR translates into sales volume, and this isn't a fixed value anyway.

However, a number of people (myself included) have recorded their own sales volume and corresponding sales rank. There are also a few online tools that can give estimates. The problem for me is that some of these online tools don't correlate very well with what I have seen from my own book sales.

Here are estimates based on my own book sales. The first number is the Amazon Best Sellers Rank and the number in brackets is the number of books sold in a 24-hour period.

50,000 (0-1)

30,000 (2-3)

20,000 (4-5)

10,000 (8-10)

5,000 (20-25)

4,000 (30-34)

So, if you have a sales rank of 10,000, chances are you are selling around 8 - 10 books a day. With a sales rank of around 5,000, that number jumps to 20-25 sales per day. These numbers are only estimates based on my own sales and they are far more conservative than you will get with online BSR calculators you can find online.

I can only guess at sales volume for sellers ranks better than 4,000. After reading other people's experiences, I'd expect something like this:

1,000 (100)

500 (200)

1 (3000+)

Again, I need to repeat that these figures are based on educated guesswork and listening to other authors.

Using the information in this section, you can estimate how many sales a particular book makes. If your competitor is making good sales, then you know there is a market for books on that topic.

As an example, that zombie book has a BSR of 3,386. That translates into around 40 sales a day. Multiply that by the royalty rate the book gets, and you can estimate how much money the author is making.

Potential profits from book sales

When you sell a book on Amazon Kindle, Amazon pays you a royalty.

The value of the royalty is a percentage of the sale after any deductions for download bandwidth. The fee Amazon charges for each download of your book depends on the size of your book in megabytes (MB). You won't get charged this fee on smaller books (or free books), but as the book size increases, Amazon starts to deduct a delivery fee out of the purchase price.

Before we look at delivery costs, it's important to understand the royalty structure. This can also change, so for the most up-to-date information, do check with Amazon.

There are two Royalty "options" - 70% or 35%.

If your book is priced between $2.99 and $9.99, then you are eligible for 70% royalties, except in certain circumstances. For example, sales in certain countries will only result in 35% royalties. However, to complicate things, 70% royalties may be possible in some countries, but only if your book is enrolled in KDP. We'll discuss KDP later in the promotion section.

If your book outside that price range (higher or lower), then you get 35% royalties on all sales. There are no download fees on books where the royalty is 35%.

On sales that qualify for the 70% royalty, there may be a download charge. The charge is similar in all countries and in the US, is equal to $0.15 per MB at the time of writing. Therefore, if your book is 3MB in size (which it might be if you have a lot of images or photos), then the delivery charge on each sale that is eligible for 70% royalties will be 3 x $0.15 = $0.45.

For more details on book pricing and royalties, see these pages on Amazon:

1. Pricing Page: https://goo.gl/t7e222

2. Sales & Royalties FAQ: https://goo.gl/FnJPtF

For now, your next step is to write your book. In the following section, we'll look at how you should format your book.

Writing & formatting your book

You can use pretty much any software tool for writing your book, including any of the free Office Suites like Open Office, Libre Office, etc. There is also a software tool, written specifically for authors; it's called Scrivener. There are Windows and Mac versions of Scrivener and it makes formatting extremely easy, but there is a learning curve. Using Scrivener, it's actually quite difficult to make a mess of your book when it's time to compile and upload it.

Download links:

Open Office - http://www.openoffice.org/

Libre Office – http://www.libreoffice.org/

Scrivener - http://www.literatureandlatte.com/

Obviously, I cannot cover details of all these tools, so I'll stick with Microsoft Word for this book, and if you own it, you should use it to write your first book. If you are using one of the free Office Tools, just follow along as best you can because the process is very similar for each word processor.

If you are an experienced word processor user, then a lot of the formatting we do in this book will seem obvious. That's OK, but don't skip this section as there are some basic formatting styles you need to adhere to for electronic books.

Creating a style for your books

Before I started publishing books on Kindle and Createspace, I set up a Word "Style" that could accommodate how I wanted to do things. You can do a very similar process in any Word processor.

I'll show you how to set this up in Microsoft Word.

If you are fairly new to Word and don't have a preferred setup in terms of fonts, paragraphs, alignment, margins, etc., then I suggest you start off by selecting one of the presets built into Word and modify that.

You can do this by clicking on the **Design** tab.

There are a number of ready-made document formatting styles that you can select. There are also a number of different **Themes** that you can choose.

Let me show you how to set this up.

From the **Themes** menu, select **Office.**

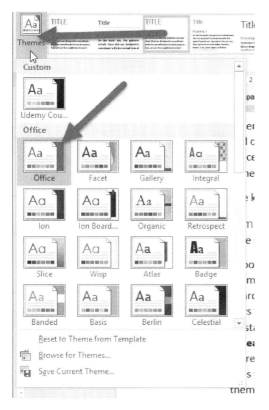

Each theme in that list will load its own unique set of document formatting styles, which you can view by mousing over them in the **Document Formatting** window:

As your mouse moves from one to the next, the text in your Word document will update to show you that style. You will also get a tooltip to tell you the name of the style you are viewing.

Select the **Black & White (Word).**

This gives us a starting point to create our own style.

Which Font?

When writing your book, stick to a plain and simple font and never mix 2 or more fonts within the same document. Amazon Kindle will over-write your font(s) anyway, but that may not be the case with other eBook publishing platforms, and it certainly isn't the case when you publish your book as a paperback. Get into the habit of using a single font throughout.

Font size is not critical for Kindle versions because Kindle owners can change the font size on their device. However, if you are going to be creating a paperback from your Word document, it is important. Therefore, I suggest you set up Word to use the correct font sized from the beginning.

If you want to read some thoughts on fonts, look at this article – Picking Fonts for your Indie Book:

https://goo.gl/JGBK7b

Please note that you can't just use any font. You need to make sure you have the rights to use the font commercially. I am not a lawyer, so please don't ask my advice on this. You need to read the copyright information of the fonts you have access to. Having said that, any fonts that came pre-installed with Word, are probably safe to use.

There are a couple of places you can find free fonts for commercial use:

1. https://www.exljbris.com/

2. https://www.fontsquirrel.com/

There is also a good site where you can buy complete pre-made Word templates for your books:

http://ezseonews.com/booktemplates

Quick Style Buttons

On the **Home** tab in Word, the ribbon bar has "buttons" for quickly selecting styles for the text of your book.

If you select any text in your Word document and click one of these buttons, the text will be formatted accordingly. Exactly what formatting is applied depends on how that style is formatted in the currently selected style.

Click the **Heading 1** button, and the selected text will become a large heading. Click on **Normal**, and your selected text will be formatted as "normal" text.

The main text in your book should be formatted to the "Normal" style:

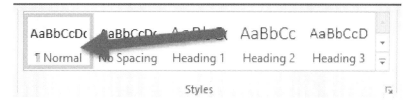

You can test this by clicking into a paragraph of your book, and the Normal format should become highlighted:

k and you have your cover. The next step is to upload your book to
y easy and all you need is an Amazon account, which I assume you

b-filtered HTML document and zipped it up ready for upload.

You can see where I have clicked into the paragraph, and the Normal format is highlighted.

The main formatting styles I use in my books are as follows:

• **Normal** – For the main text of the book.

• **No Spacing** –for problems with some justified text that tries to stretch a few words across an entire line. I set this style to left-aligned to prevent these issues.

• **Heading 1** – For chapter headings.

• **Heading 2** – For the main sub-headers in the chapter.

• **Heading 3** – For sub-sections of the main chapter sections.

• **Title** – For the title on the cover page.

• **Subtitle** – For the subtitle/tagline on the cover page.

• **Quote** – For quoting people, websites or other sources.

You need to make sure that all of these formats are set up to use your chosen font.

Quickly changing the default font for your style

We can quickly change the font used in a style by clicking the **Fonts** button over on the Design tab:

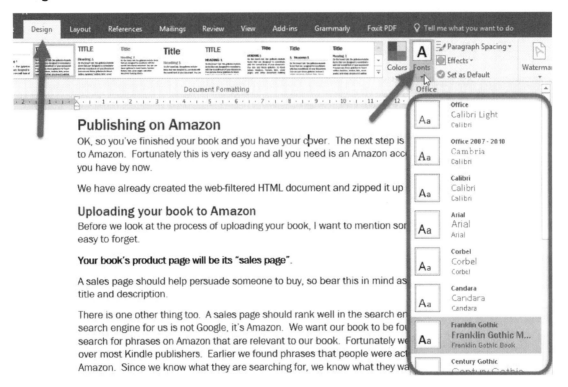

Select the font you want to use, and all styles will be updated to use that font.

For now, select the Office font, Calibri Light, at the top.

OK; all styles now use this font. However, this does not change the color or size of the text. We need to do that manually.

To do that, simply right-click on the style button you want to edit and select the **Modify** option:

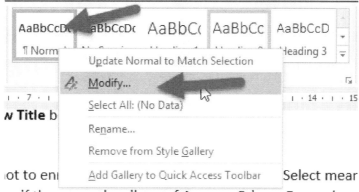

This opens a dialogue box that allows you to change the font style:

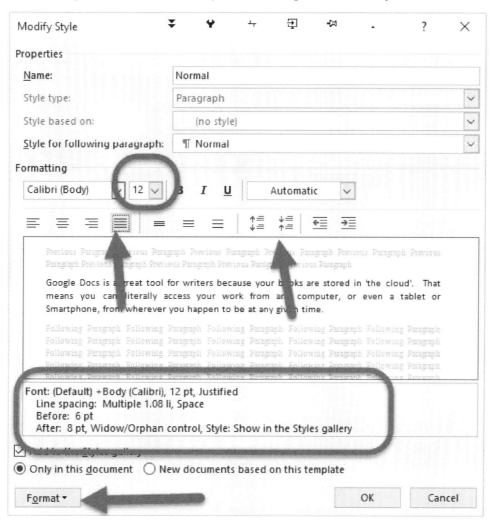

I'd recommend that **Normal** text should be no smaller than size 12.

Notice that you can also change the alignment of the text, and if you want your paragraphs justified, select the justify button. On the same toolbar, there is a button you can select to space out your paragraphs. This is how you SHOULD space your paragraphs, rather than typing in hard line breaks to leave a space.

At the bottom, you can see the format specifications as you make the changes. You can see mine now has the 12pt font, justified with line spacing set to 1.08. There is also 6pt space before each paragraph and an 8pt space after each paragraph.

These are good settings for the Normal style.

This is almost how I want my paragraphs displayed, with one small change. I want my line spacing a little more than 1.08. I want to set this as 1.15. To do this, click the Format button at the bottom left and select **Paragraph** from the menu.

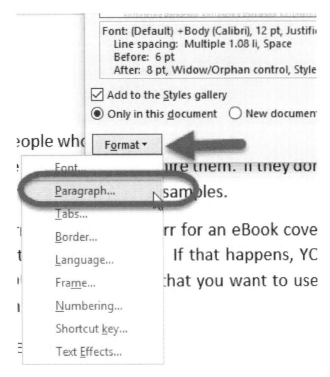

This opens up a new screen that allows us to refine the formatting.

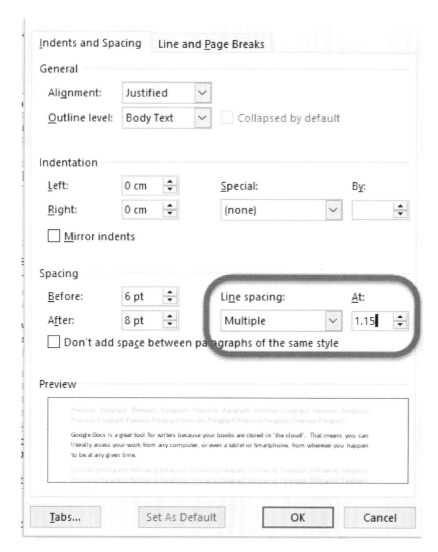

Select **Multiple** from the line spacing drop-down box and set that to 1.15.

Click OK to close this dialogue box, and OK to close the **Modify Style** screen.

We now need to set the sizes of the headers (Heading 1, Heading 2 and Heading 3 are usually the only ones I use in my books). To do this, just right-click the style button and select Modify for each header in turn.

Here are my settings for the Heading 3:

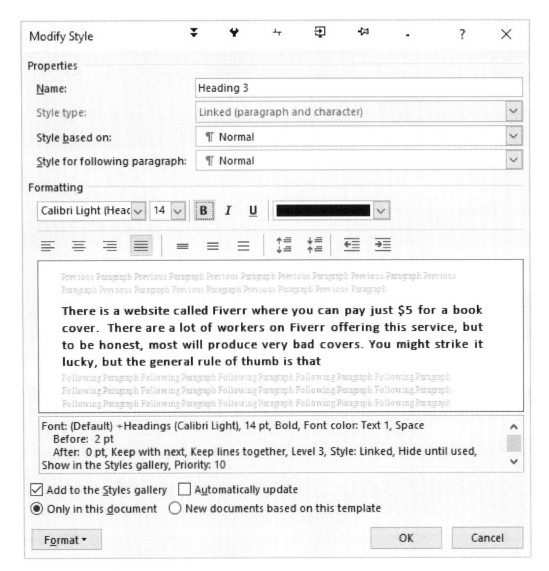

I've set the size to 14 and made the heading bold and color black.

I always add two points to my "normal" text size to use as the Heading 3. I'll then add 2 more for heading 2, and 2 more for heading 1. This is just personal preference, but here is a quick reference for those sizes:

Normal text – 12

Heading 1 - 18

Heading 2 - 16

Heading 3 - 14

Obviously, you need to decide on these for yourself and what works best with the type of book you are writing, but the headings are hierarchical, so the Heading 1 should be bigger than Heading 2 which is bigger than Heading 3. Heading 3 should be bigger than the main text to make sure the headers stand out.

OK, you can now save your style.

On the Design tab, in the bottom right corner of the **Document Formatting** options, there is a button:

Click it.

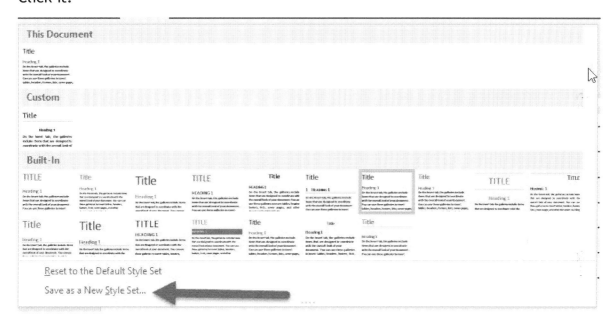

On the drop-down menu that appears, click on the **Save as a New Style Set...** option.

Give your style a name, e.g. Kindle Books and save it.

You can now see that style added to the Custom section of the menu:

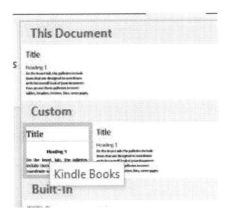

The style will now be available whenever you start a new book. Just select it, and your formatting and style options will be loaded for your new book.

If you want to format a pre-existing document, then after you load your book into Word, just go and select your style from the drop-down menu.

The Essential Sections of your Book

When you create a book, there are a few special pages that you need to include in the manuscript, either before or after the main book content. However, what you include may depend on whether your book is fiction or non-fiction. Let's look at these special pages. You can refer to the corresponding sections of this book if you want an example.

Before the Main Book Content

1. Cover Page – This page shows the title, subtitle, author, and version or release date. At the end of the cover page content, insert a page break.

2. Disclaimer and Terms of Use – a legal disclaimer that essentially disclaims liability for information in the book and confirms copyright. You can find examples if you search Google.

3. Extra Information - This can be anything you want your readers to be aware of. It might be a "How to use this book" paragraph for non-fiction books, or a list of "testimonials" you've received for the book. One bit of information I like to include is an email address with a request for readers to report typos and errors. You'll also see that this book explains why I have shortened URLs in some cases.

After the Main Book Content

1. Useful Resources – If you have resources you want to tell your readers about, include them in a resource section. This can include other books you've written, courses, websites, etc.

2. Ask for a review – Reviews are everything on Amazon. You have to be careful in how you ask, but there is nothing wrong saying something like "If you enjoyed this book, please consider leaving an honest review on Amazon".

3. An Index – If you are writing non-fiction books and plan to publish as a paperback, you might want to consider an index page. Word does have features to help you manage these, through making a useful index is a time-consuming activity. I haven't included one in the first version of this book but may consider adding one in time.

Important formatting rules

With the style setup, let's look at how we use these formatting options to create a single manuscript that can be used to generate both Kindle and Paperback versions of the book.

Headings

The types of headings you will include in your book vary, depending on the type of book you are writing. If you are a fiction writer, then headings may be limited to Chapter headings and possibly a few other sections in the book, like "About the Author", or "More books by the author".

If you are a non-fiction writer, headings are usually nested. Typically, each chapter will start with a large header (heading 1) and may then be broken down into sub-sections, each with their own heading (heading 2).

In Word Processors, headers are usually defined by a number. Header 1 is the largest, then header 2, header 3, header 4 and so on.

All main section headings in your book (like the start of each chapter) should be the Header 1 level (the largest).

If you divide your main sections into smaller sections, then these should be Level 2. Any sub-headings within the sub-headings should be level 3. I probably wouldn't go deeper than 3 nested levels.

Adding headings in your book is easy. Simply select the text you want to change to a heading, and click on the heading style you want from the **Styles** selector:

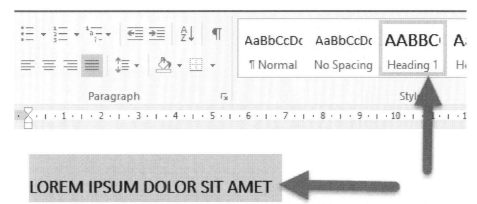

In other word processors, this may look a little different. In Libre Office, for example, it looks like this:

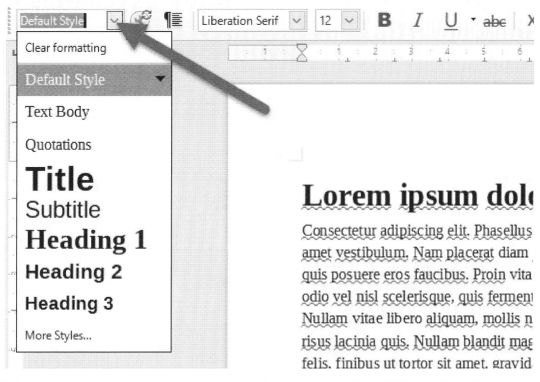

The process of creating a heading is the same in Libre Office. You first select the text and then set the formatting by choosing it from this drop-down style box.

Paragraphs, carriage returns, and page breaks

When it comes to paragraphs and carriage returns, there is a very important rule. This rule is easier to explain if you turn "Show/Hide" hidden formatting ON:

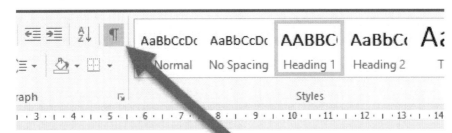

This will show non-printing formatting symbols that are otherwise hidden in the word processor. For example, you should see the pilcrow symbol whenever you press the return (enter) key to move onto the next line:

This·will·show·non-printing·formatting·symbols·that·are
processor.°·For·example,·you·should·see·the·pilcrow·s
return·(enter)·key·to·move·onto·the·next·line:¶

¶

NOTE:·°The·pilcrow·symbol·may·already·be·visible·in·you
the·visual·formatting·on.°·¶

It·is·very·important·to·see·these·characters·because·the

The·rule·I·want·to·give·you·is·this:¶

NOTE: The pilcrow symbol may already be visible in your editor without having to turn the visual formatting on.

It is very important to see these characters because they represent hard line breaks.

The rule I want to give you is this:

Never have a hard line break on an empty line.

Here is what that looks like:

processor. ° For·example, ·you·should·see·the·pilcrow·s
return·(enter)·key·to·move·onto·the·next·line:¶

¶

NOTE: · The·pilcrow·symbol·may·already·be·visible·in·yo
the·visual·formatting·on. ° ¶

It·is·very·important·to·see·these·characters·because·the

You should only see the hard line breaks at the end of each paragraph (the pilcrow symbol). If you can see them on their own, between paragraphs, you should delete them. Having hard line breaks between paragraphs will create a very big space between them on Kindle devices. If you have any of these "stranded" symbols throughout your document, remove them.

Just to recap then, when you are writing a paragraph, finish it, hit the return key ONCE, and then immediately start typing the next paragraph. There will be a visible gap between the two paragraphs in Word, which is added by the formatting we set up for the **Normal** style.

If you follow this rule, you should not get into a mess with the spacing of your documents when they are converted into a Kindle book format. If you know this rule, it should be obvious that you NEVER use the return key (hard line breaks) to space out content.

If you need something to start on a new page (e.g. a new chapter), create a page break

Page breaks

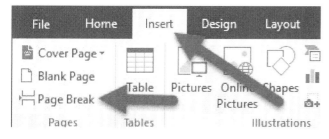

The correct way to insert a page break in your document is to go to the Insert tab and click the **Page Break** button.

The keyboard shortcut on a PC for a page break is CTRL + Enter key.

If text MUST start on a new page, then insert a page break directly before that text.

For example, use page breaks at the end of a chapter, so that the new chapter starts on a fresh page.

Hyperlinks

The newer generations of Kindle readers (plus the Kindle reading software on iPads, PCs, Macs, Android devices & iPhones), can all read and follow hyperlinks to external websites. If you want to link out to a website, you just create the hyperlink in MS Word by selecting the text you want to use for the link and then right-click on the selected area. You then choose "Link" from the popup menu that appears:

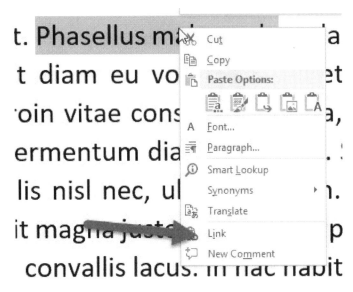

This opens a dialogue box:

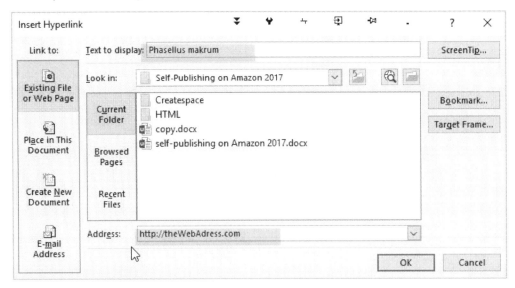

At the top, you can see the text that will be displayed in the link (link text), and the address box at the bottom is where you type in the website address you want that text linked to.

Click on the OK button to insert the link into the document.

However, if you are intending to create a paperback version of your book, then there is no point having a link like this.

The reader will see the word underlined (the link) but have no idea where it goes. Therefore, as I have done in this book, if you want to link to a website, use the full URL (or a shortened version).

Lists

When Amazon converts a book to the Kindle format, it sometimes does not display bullet lists correctly. If you have a problem with this when you convert your book, be aware that you can insert bullet symbols manually to make sure you get the formatting you want.

To create a bullet (on a PC), hold down the ALT key while you type in 0149.

That creates a bullet like this: •

You can then just type bullets in manually. Here is a bullet list created this way:

• manual bullet item 1

• manual bullet item 2

• manual bullet item 3

Word's **numbered lists** do convert OK, so you can use those without worry. However, do make sure each new list starts at the correct number (usually 1) and isn't simply continuing numbering where the last list finished. I've had a lot of problems with this, so avoid numbered lists as well, and just type the numbers manually.

Images

Images are important in certain types of books. You can easily add images into your book by inserting them into the Word document where you want them to appear. However, there are a few things to be aware of:

Image size

Images take up physical space on a disk drive. The larger the file size, the larger your final Word document will be. Since Amazon charges a download fee on bigger books, you want to keep your Word document size as small as possible. It is, therefore, a good idea to correctly size and compress your images so that they take up less space.

NOTE: If you are using MS Word, it has a built-in feature to compress pictures when you save your document. That means you can create a single Word document with high-resolution images, and save it in two formats when publishing. One for the paperback with high-resolution images, and the other for Kindle with lower resolution images. However, you should correctly size your images before you insert them into your document.

First, decide how big your paperback version will be and work out the size of the "content rectangle" that will hold the content of your book. To do that, we need to know page size and margins.

Here is a screenshot of a page from this book, with the content rectangle highlighted.

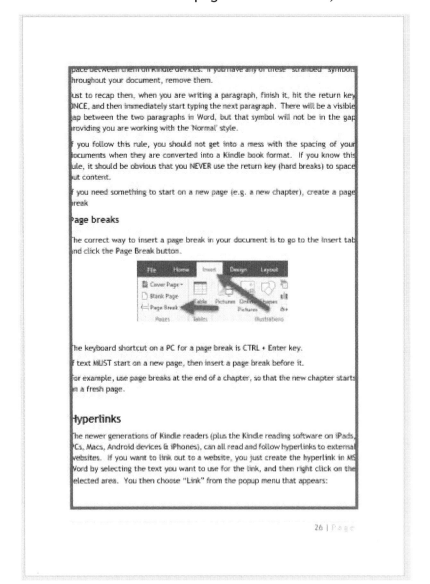

On the Layout tab in Word, you can check your document's size:

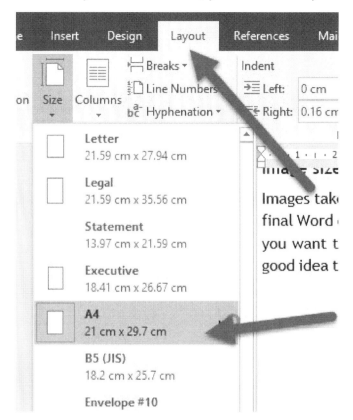

For this book, my document size is 21cm wide by 29.7cm tall.

To find the margin, there is a button on the Layout tab which will tell you what you need to know:

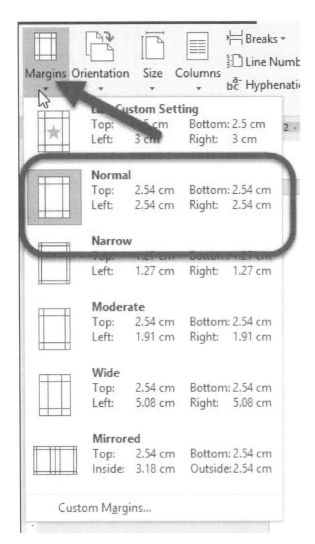

So, my page is 21cm wide, with margins on the left and right of 2.54cm each. That means the width of my content rectangle is 21cm – 2.54cm – 2.54cm = 15.92cm.

I can work out the height of my content rectangle using the same information. Therefore, the content rectangle of my book is 15.92cm x 24.62cm.

With that information, I can correctly size an image before it is inserted into the document. If I want an image to take up the full width of a page, but only half the height, then the image should be 15.92cm x 12.31cm.

It will then take up the appropriate space in my document:

Be aware that if you insert an image that is too small, Word will allow you to stretch it. However, avoid doing this because the resulting image can become very "pixely". Resize the image to the correct size before inserting, and you'll be fine.

How to insert an image

Inserting images can be done in a couple of ways. The first method is to copy the image from your graphics software and paste it into the Word document. I have heard other Kindle authors having problems with this method, but it seems to work fine for me. The other way to insert an image (and most Kindle authors recommend you do it this way), is by clicking on the **Insert** tab of the ribbon bar, and then clicking on the **Pictures** button.

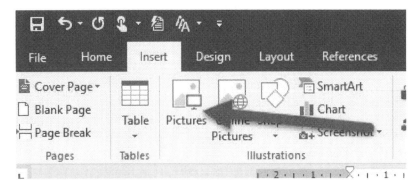

You'll be shown an image selection dialogue box, so choose your image and click the Insert button to insert it into your document.

Color images v black & white

I recommend you use full-color images in your Word document.

Some Kindles (as well as tablets & Smartphones) have color displays and it is nice to have images in color as you read a book. Many traditional Kindles are black and white only, and they will convert your images to black and white for you, so you don't need to.

I'd recommend you check when you preview your book at the time of upload to see whether all of your images are visible in the auto-converted B&W as well as color. If any images are unclear, just redo them.

Page numbers

Kindle devices allow the reader to change the text size of the book they are reading.   Because of this, the page you see in Word will not necessarily be a full page on the Kindle device. What you see in your Word document as page 5, for example, may well be page 10 on a Kindle.   We, therefore, do not include page numbers in the Kindle format of the book.

However, the way we will save the Word document for the Kindle version will strip out page numbers for us if they are in the document. If you are intending to publish your book as a paperback, then add page numbers now.

Page Numbering in Word

I like Word, but I also hate it for making things so complicated. Something that should be as easy as adding page numbers to a document, is a process that takes a little figuring out.

Step-by-step instructions

Click at the top of the page where you want to start your page numbering.

On the **Layout** tab of the ribbon bar, click **Breaks** and select **Continuous** from the list:

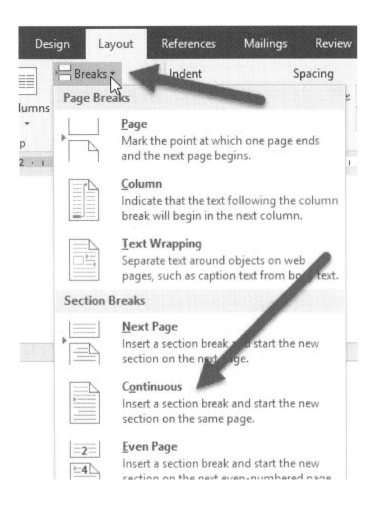

On the **Insert** tab of the ribbon bar, click **Page Number** and move your mouse down to **Bottom of Page**, and select the position where you want page numbers to appear.

Word will show you the **Design** tab active in the ribbon bar. In the **Navigation** section, DESELECT the **Link to Previous** button.

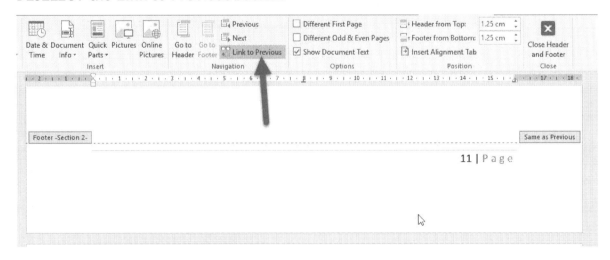

Scroll back in your Word document to the previous page (the one before your continuous page break, and click into the Footer section of the page to select it:

Now click the **Footer** button in the **Header & Footer** section of the ribbon bar at the top:

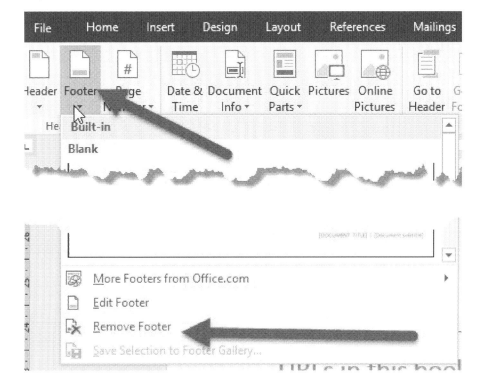

Select **Remove Footer.**

Now click on the **Close Header and Footer** button:

Click again on the page of your document where you want page numbers to begin.

Go back to the **Insert** tab, and click **Page Number, Format Page Number**:

Select **Start at:** and enter 1 in the box.

Click OK to save.

Double click somewhere on your document to get out of the edit mode.

Your page numbering should now start at 1, on the page you specified. There should be no page numbering on pages before this "first page".

Table of contents

Your book needs a table of contents whether you are creating just a Kindle version, or a paperback as well.

Let me show you how to insert a table of contents into your book.

Word has a special feature to automatically insert a table of contents (TOC). Scroll to the place in your document where you want the TOC to appear. Now add a page break so that your TOC will begin on its own page.

Click on the **References** tab in Word's ribbon bar and then click on the **Table of Contents** button:

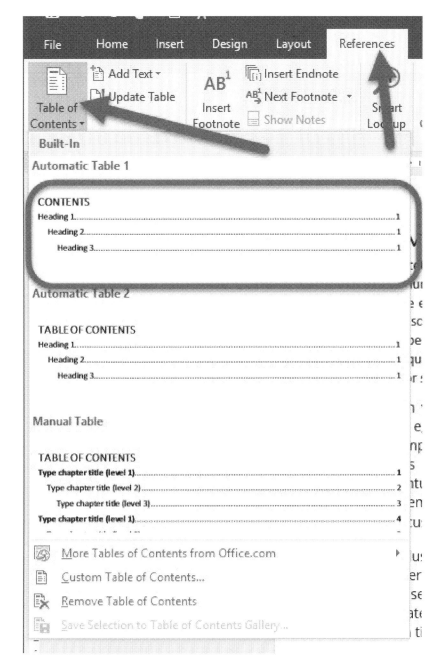

All of the "Built-In" TOC styles contain page numbers, but that is fine as they will be used by the paperback and stripped out of the Kindle when we save this document in the two separate formats.

Just click on the TOC you want, and it will be inserted into your document.

We now need to insert a bookmark at the start of the TOC, so that Kindle devices can "GoTo TOC". This is easy enough.

Move your cursor to the start of the table of contents title (click just before the title starts), and then on the **Insert menu** on the ribbon bar, select **Bookmark**.

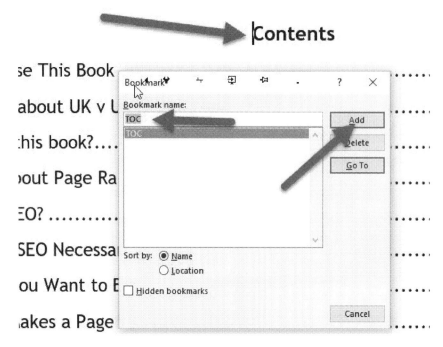

Type TOC as the bookmark name, and then click the Add button.

This will add a bookmark that Kindle readers can access.

NOTE: If someone complains that your book does not have this feature, Kindle may remove your book from the marketplace until you add it, so it's important to do it now.

After the last entry in your TOC, insert a page break. This ensures that the next section of your book does not begin on the same page as the final entries of your TOC.

Updating a TOC

As you work on your book, you may add new sections, or arrange and delete other parts. You'll probably want to update the table of contents as you go along. This is very easy.

Right-click any entry in the TOC, and select **Update Field** from the menu.

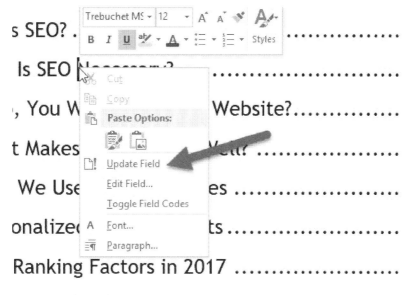

A dialogue box appears with two options:

Word is updating the table of contents. Select one
of the following options:
- ◉ Update page numbers only
- ○ Update entire table

[OK]   [Cancel]

You can either update the whole table or just the page numbers. If you've added and deleted sections in your book, update the whole table to be sure they are inserted into the TOC.

Previewing your book

You'll actually want to preview your book when you upload it to Amazon to ensure everything is OK. However, as you write your book, you can also check how it will look using the free Kindle Previewer software available from Amazon.

Previewer download URL:

https://goo.gl/krE3Ze

Download and install it (there are Windows and Mac versions). I'll be showing you the Windows version so it may look a little different if you are on a Mac.

The Kindle Previewer only works with a few file formats which do not include Word's or Open Office's native formats. Accepted formats are Mobi, ePub, HTML, and OPF.

The easiest thing to do is to save your book as HTML using Word's **Web Page, Filtered** format. This is the same format we'll use to upload the finished book to Amazon, and I have found that this format is the most reliable.

Saving as Web Page, Filtered

Before doing anything else, save your document in Word's DOC or DOCX format.

With that saved, you can now create the HTML version of the file.

You can do this in Word by selecting **Save As**.

In the dialogue box that opens, choose the **Web Page, Filtered** option.

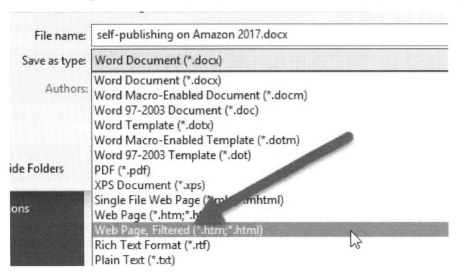

Don't click the Save button yet as we need to make sure image size is reduced.

Click on the **Tools** button, and select **Web Options**.

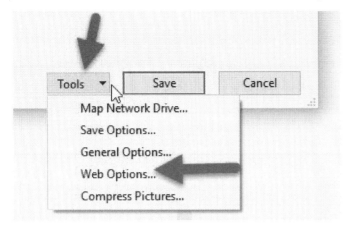

This opens a screen showing web options (web options because we are saving as a web page):

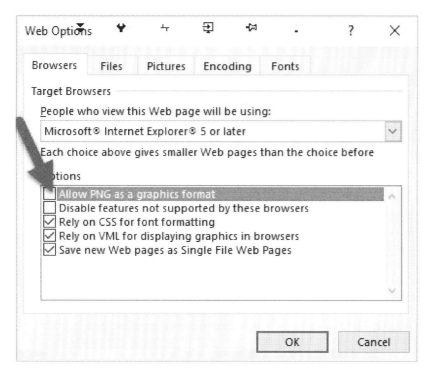

The important options here is the top one. Make sure **Allow PNG as a graphic format** is disabled.

Now click on the **Pictures** tab:

This is where you can specify image size. I would recommend the above settings, but if you find your book file is still too large, reduce the pixels per inch to 72. You could also reduce screen size.

Once done, click on the OK button, and save your file.

When you do that, the active document in Word will be the newly created web page filtered version of your book. Since we want to load this document into the Kindle Previewer, we first need to close it in Word.

Do that now. Close your Word document.

OK, open the Kindle Previewer software:

Welcome

Kindle Previewer is a graphical user interface tool that emulates

Announcements

Amazon has launched the new Kindle Previewer 3 (Beta) to pre Launch" _here_ .

Open Book to preview *
* Files Supported: MOBI, EPUB, HTML, OPF

Open Recent Files...

Click the **Open Book** link and navigate to where you saved the HTML version of your book.

You'll get a dialogue box saying that your document is being compiled. Wait for this to finish and you should get a confirmation box like this one:

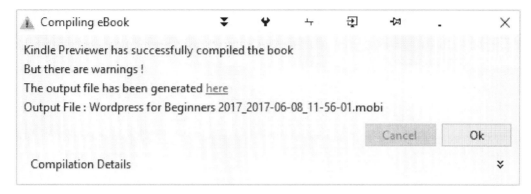

If you get a message saying the conversion failed, check to make sure you closed the copy of your document in the word processor, and try again.

When you click the OK button on the compile confirmation screen, the preview window should open, displaying your book.

WordPress for Beginners 2017

A Visual Step-by-Step Guide to Mastering Wordpress

Updated June 5th 2017

Across the top of the previewer window is a menu item called **Devices**. This allows you to change the emulator so that you can see what your book looks like on other reading devices.

It is worth going through every page of your document to check that the formatting and general layout looks OK. In particular, check any images you have in your document. Are your images clear? If not, you might want to redo them.

If you are happy, zip it up.

When you are happy with your book format, you need to create the zip file that we will upload later to Amazon during the submission process.

When Word saved your document as web page filtered HTML, it saved the main book file as an HTML file in your chosen folder. It also created a folder inside this folder to store all images in your book.

The next step is to zip-up the HTML document, and all of the images, into a single zip file.

There are a lot of different zip tools available, so I cannot show you exactly how to do this. However, if you have a zip program installed on your computer such as WinZip, then you can create the zip file quickly and easily from Windows File Explorer.

Select both the HTML file and the folder containing the images.

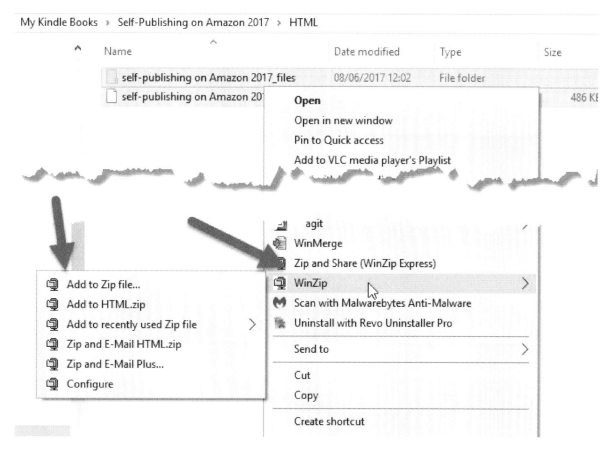

Right click on the highlighted files, and you should see a link to your zip software in the popup menu that appears. In my screenshot, I am using WinZip. If I move my mouse down to WinZip, a second menu appears with a top option to **Add to Zip file**. By clicking that, WinZip effortlessly creates my zip file, all ready for uploading to Amazon.

If you open the zip file that you have just created, you should see the HTML file and the folder containing your images.

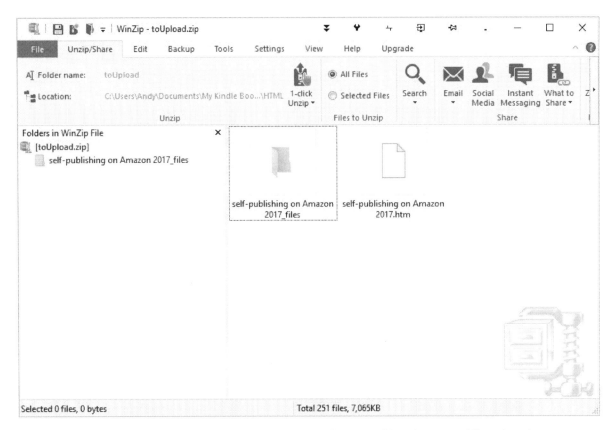

When you submit your book to Amazon, it is this zip file that you'll upload.

What about Google Docs?

Google Docs is a great tool for writers because your books are stored in the cloud. That means you can literally access your work from any computer, or even a tablet or Smartphone, from wherever you happen to be at any given time.

To upload a book to Amazon that was written in Google docs, download the book as a web page zip file and then upload that zip file to Amazon.

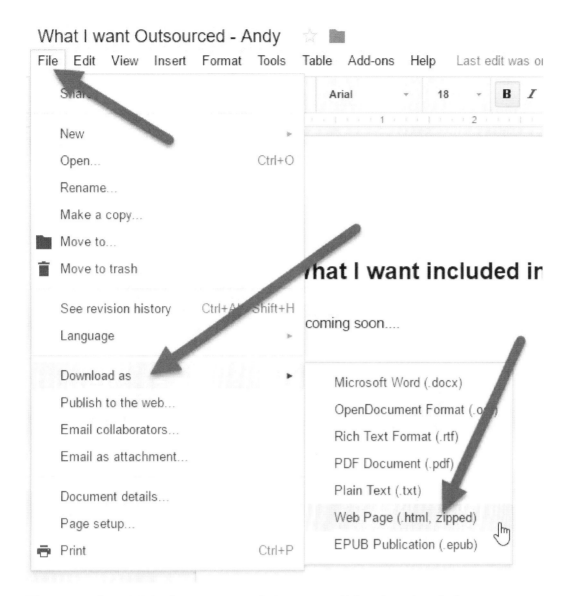

The zipped-up Web document with images will be downloaded to your computer.

Editor v DIY Proofing

Trying to proofread your own book is difficult. You tend to read what should be there, rather than what actually is. In addition, if your own command of language isn't 100%, then you are working on a rocky foundation.

If you can afford it, I highly recommend you hire someone to go through your book and correct spelling and grammar. It doesn't require a full editor, just someone that knows their grammar.

If you cannot afford to hire a professional, then use family and friends. I also recommend you look up Grammarly.

Grammarly is an online grammar and spelling service that offers both free and paid accounts. It also has an add-on for Word that can offer suggestions for grammar and spelling, even if you only have a free Grammarly account.

https://www.grammarly.com/office-addin/

Once installed, Grammarly adds a button to your ribbon bar:

Clicking on that button opens up the Grammarly sidebar which offers suggestions on your Word document:

e you been searching for in

our friends and your circles.

ce, desktop or even SmartTV.

ce our lives easier, and in many
rsonalization can be a pain if we
's.

optimise → optimize

friends,

Missing comma in a series

Your sentence contains a series of three or more words,
phrases, or clauses. Consider inserting a comma to separate
the elements.

⌄ MORE   ✕ IGNORE

⟳ checking...

In this case, Grammarly wants to add a comma after the word "friends". It's important
to check your text to see whether the suggestion is correct. If it is correct, click on
the correction to make the change in your Word document.

friends,

Missing comma in a series

Your sentence contains a series of three or more
phrases, or clauses. Consider inserting a comma
the elements.

This Grammarly check is something I recommend you do for all your books. Wait until
you think the book is ready to publish, then go through it with this Grammarly plugin
to catch the final few errors.

Kindle book covers

Book covers are the main way Kindle authors get their foot in the door. When someone is searching Amazon, it's the first thing they see. If your cover sucks, people are less likely to click through and read your description or reviews, as they'll assume the book is equally as bad as the cover. Of course, if your cover is bad, you probably won't have many reviews anyway. It is therefore VITAL for your success that your covers look professional. Remember, when it comes to selling eBooks, you never get a second chance to make a first impression.

I'd recommend you think of your cover as a headline. You need to use it to get people clicking through to your "sales letter" (the book's product page on Amazon with description and reviews).

Have a look through the Kindle section on Amazon and see what it is that makes some covers appear more professional than others. Look specifically at covers in your niche or genre. Are there any that stand out to you? Why do you like them, what is it that makes them so special? What types of fonts are being used on great looking book covers? What about book covers that look "cheap"? What about colors and layout etc.?

Do they use photos or images? If so, do the images correlate well with the topic of the book? Do the images make you want to click through to the product page?

NOTE: If you want to use a photo on your cover, you need to make sure you have the rights to include the image. The best way to do that is to buy the image license from a stock photo site like iStockPhoto or PhotoDune. I tend to use Photodune as they are cheaper.

iStockPhoto – http://www.istockphoto.com/

PhotoDune - http://photodune.net/

There are some "eBook cover designer" tools that promise to help you make professional looking covers quickly and easily. I personally don't rate them and think the results look quite poor. A good graphics program (I use Paint Shop Pro X9) is far better if you have a few skills.

Obviously, designing a book cover is beyond the scope of this book. However, if you want to try it yourself, here are a couple of web pages that offer good advice:

- https://goo.gl/JcVHh2

- https://goo.gl/Z5UUTa

Here are a few things to think about:

1. Make sure that the cover looks good in black & white as well as color. Don't forget that older Kindle's are B&W and that is how those readers will see your cover on Amazon.

2. Use professional images (e.g. like photos from the sources mentioned earlier), but *don't use photos that look like typical stock photos* (if that makes sense). If you look through a few stock photos of people, you'll understand what I mean. Also, remember that you don't have to use the full photo (crop it) and you can rotate it vertically to make it "back-to-front". With graphics tools like Paint Shop Pro, Photoshop, or even free tools, you can add effects to these images so be creative.

3. Use a large, clear font for your title so that it's visible in the thumbnail (in color and black & white).

4. Don't mix fonts on your cover. Choose one (or at most 2), that looks good and stick with it. Don't use fancy, curly fonts unless you're in the romance niche, as it can work there, but even then, do check that your title can be read as a thumbnail.

5. Check out https://goo.gl/C5aiG7 for guidance on your cover. To summarize the main points of that web page, the image should be a .jpeg or .tiff. Dimensions should be a minimum of 625 pixels on its shortest side and 1,000 pixels on the longest side. However, bigger is better and Amazon recommends 1600 on the shortest side, with 2,560 on the longest side.

6. Check out your cover as a thumbnail image by shrinking it down so that the longest side of the image is just 200 - 220 pixels. Amazon actually uses different sized thumbnails in various places on the site. Can you read the important text in the thumbnail?

7. Be mindful of the fact that you won't get a second chance to make that first impression.

Where to get "professional" covers done for you?

Professional covers can work out very expensive. I'm talking about hundreds of dollars here. There are some cheaper alternatives out there, but the cheaper the cover, the more likely you are to be disappointed.

The cheapest option

There is a website called Fiverr where you can pay just $5 for a book cover. There are a lot of workers on Fiverr offering this service, but to be honest, most will produce very bad covers. You might strike it lucky, but the general rule of thumb is that you get what you pay for. My biggest worry about using Fiverr for an eBook cover is that the contractor you hire may use images that violate copyright. If that happens, YOU are liable, not the contractor. I'd recommend YOU buy any images that you want to use on your cover and give them to the person designing your cover.

A little more expensive

There are a few sites out there that offer pre-made covers you can buy for a reasonable price. Here are a few:

- http://www.coverkicks.com

- http://Litteradesigns.com

- http://www.goonwrite.com

- http://authormarketingclub.com

Whoever you hire to create your cover, ask them about the copyright on any images they have used on the cover. Ideally, you should ask them about this BEFORE you hire them for the job ;)

Higher priced covers

Perhaps one of the best places to get an eBook cover designed for you is on 99 Designs:

https://99designs.co.uk

This site allows you to setup a "competition" to design your cover for as little as £229.

Designers will create designs and offer them for your consideration. You only pay for a design if you use it, and there is no obligation to use any of the designs created.

The good thing is, you can get the design for the paperback book, and use the "front cover" of that for the eBook cover. That way to get both covers designed professionally for the one price. Here is a book cover I got designed on 99 Designs:

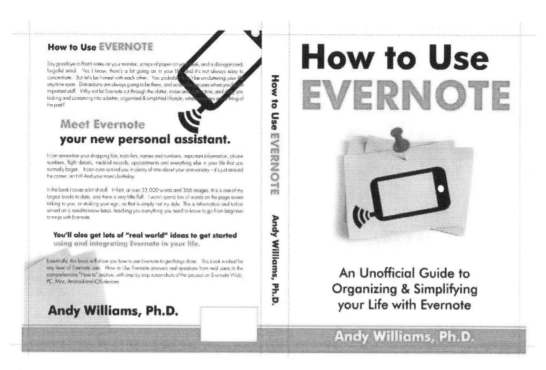

That is the paperback cover, and with a little editing, I can use the front section of the cover for the Kindle version.

Publishing on Amazon

OK, so you've finished your book and you have your cover. The next step is to upload your book to Amazon. Fortunately, this is very easy and all you need is an Amazon account, which I assume you have by now.

We have already created the web-filtered HTML document and zipped it up ready for upload.

Uploading your book to Amazon

Before we look at the process of uploading your book, I want to mention something that is all too easy to forget.

Your book's product page will be its "sales page".

A sales page should help persuade someone to buy, so bear this in mind as you write the book's title and description.

There is one other thing too. A sales page should rank well in the search engines. The important search engine for us is not Google, it's Amazon. We want our book to be found when people search for phrases on Amazon that are relevant to our book. Fortunately, we've got an advantage over most Kindle publishers. Earlier we found phrases that people were actually searching for on Amazon. Since we know what they are searching for, we know what they want, so we can tailor our sales page to give it to them.

To help our book appear for the terms that people are searching for, it helps if the sales page includes relevant phrases within it.

There are three sections that allow you to enter these keywords when you submit your book – the title, the description, and the search keywords. By using all three areas, we can get a leg-up the ranking ladder.

If you are a fiction writer, chances are you won't want to put keywords into your title, so you'll depend more on the description and search keywords.

If you are a non-fiction writer, you may be able to naturally add keywords into the title.

OK, let's publish.

Head on over to the Kindle Direct Publishing web page - https://kdp.amazon.com

Sign in with your Amazon account

Sign in

Not Andy?
Click here to sign in as different user.

You will be signed in using our secure server

If you don't have an Amazon account, sign up for one from this screen, otherwise **Sign In** and you'll be taken to your "Bookshelf".

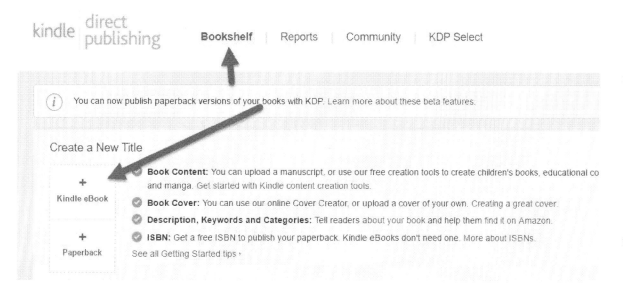

To start the process of adding your new book, click the "**+ Kindle eBook**" button. You'll be taken to the Kindle eBook Details form.

The first thing you need to enter is the language for your book, so select the language from the drop-down menu:

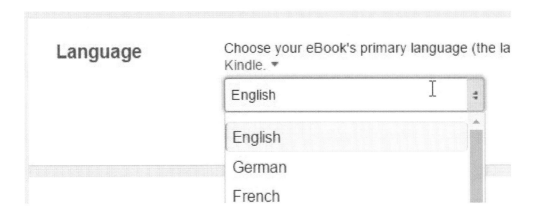

The book title

You need to enter the title of your book, but there is space for an optional subtitle:

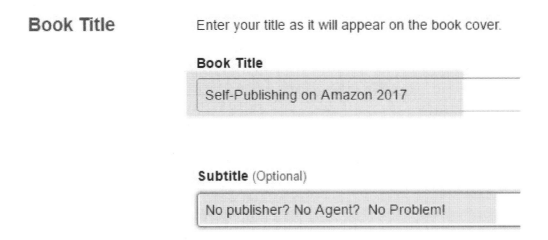

The title of the book is really important for two reasons:

1. People will read the title and decide there and then if they want to click through to your product page to read the description and reviews. Does the title convince them that this book is what they are looking for?

2. Keywords in the title will help your book rank on Amazon. Obviously the higher it ranks when someone searches Amazon, the more chance there is that people will see your book.

Make sure that the title you enter matches the actual title on your book cover. Amazon doesn't want any kind of keyword trickery going on.

For non-fiction writers, the title offers a great opportunity for a little SEO. That is, if you can insert one or two important keywords into the title, your book will be given a ranking boost whenever anyone on Amazon searches for those phrases. However, make sure the title does not look stuffed with phrases as that will put off potential buyers. Make the title read well for humans first and foremost. I like to include the main keywords in the title, and then choose something a little catchier for the subtitle.

For fiction authors, you can be more relaxed about your title, but you do need a strong cover. The cover design and title need to tell the visitors on Amazon what your book is about. If you can get their attention, you can get them to click through and read your book description. Obviously, it would also help to get a keyword phrase into the title, but that is far more difficult with fiction. What I suggest you do is ignore the keyword phrases and choose a title that you like and one which will get visitors interested in getting more details about your book. You can still insert the keywords into the description and search keywords section of the submission form.

Is your book part of a series?

This is optional. If your book is part of a series, you can enter a series name and number. For example, a lot of my books are written for webmasters (people that own a website), so I have a "Webmaster" series, with each book (SEO, CSS, Wordpress, etc.) being given a different number.

The book edition number

Next up on the form is the space for an edition number.

The Edition number can help track version changes and is totally optional. It's probably more important for non-fiction writers where books are more likely to be updated over time. The first time you publish the book you'd give it an Edition number of 1. If you do an update, you can increment that number to 2, and then 3, etc.

Author

Enter your first name and last name in the boxes provided. The author name should exactly match the name used on your book cover and within the book itself.

If you have a title or letters after your name, you can add these.

A title would go before your first name in the first name box. Letters after your name would be included at the end of your surname in the Last Name box.

This is what these look like in the author section:

Primary Author or Contributor

| Andrew | | Williams, Ph.D |

or

Primary Author or Contributor

| Dr. Andrew | | Williams |

A note about pen names

It is OK to use a pen name for your writing. In fact, if you are writing fiction, I'd recommend it so that no one will actually know your true identity. You'll build up that persona through the channels we'll discuss later in the book.

If like me, you are writing non-fiction in an area where you have some authority, it makes sense to use your real name.

If there are other contributors to your book that you want to include, you can add these in the next section.

Contributors

This is where you can enter the name(s) of the people that contributed to the book. Other authors, editors, photographers, illustrators, etc. This is optional.

If you want to add contributors, select the type of contribution made, and then add their first and last name.

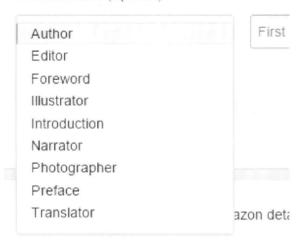

You can add additional contributors by clicking the Add Another button, which then opens up the second row.

You can remove contributors using the Remove button next to the contributor you want to remove.

The book description

The next box on the submission form is the book description. The description needs to pre-sell the visitor and you have 4000 characters to do it.

You should bear in mind that the words you type into your description will help Amazon rank your book in their search results. Remember that list of keywords you collected earlier? Try to get some of them into your description. At the same time, you don't want the description to look unnatural so make sure you write naturally. If you cannot get a keyword in, then leave it out.

Your description should tell the visitor what the book is about so they can make an informed buying decision, but don't give everything away.

If you are a fiction writer, you want the visitor to be drawn into the story by presenting some of the details but without giving too much away. Try to create an image in their mind that excites them, shocks them, or creates some form of strong emotion. You want to draw them in enough so that they want to find out what happens further in your story.

If you are struggling with this, watch a few movie trailers. Note how the movie producers make the film look exciting but without giving away the full story? This is what you need to do.

For non-fiction books, the visitors need two things. Firstly, they need to know whether the book will answer their questions. You, therefore, need to include precise details of what the book covers. The second important point is that the visitor needs to know they can trust you. They need to know that YOU know what you are talking about. If you have specific skills or qualifications related to your book, add that information to the description. If you are an online expert with a website, give the name of that website so they can go and check you out.

The description box does not give you any options for formatting your description because Amazon really doesn't want you to fiddle with formatting. I presume it's because it's very easy to end up with a mess, leaving your product page looking very unprofessional (and that doesn't look good for Amazon).

Publishing rights

The next part of the submission form is to verify your publishing rights:

⦿ I own the copyright and I hold the necessary publishing rights. What are publishing rights? ▾

◯ This is a public domain work. What is a public domain work? ▾

This is where you tell Amazon that your book is either a public domain work, or a book that you wrote (or had written), and therefore own the publishing rights. If you wrote the book, or you had a writer create the book for you, select the first option "I own the copyright and I hold the necessary publishing rights".

Keywords

Earlier when we were researching on Amazon, we used the auto-complete feature to find relevant keywords related to our book. We also did a little research on competitor books, so may have found keywords in their book titles and descriptions. It's now time to put those keywords to good use. You see, Amazon actually wants you to tell them what phrases your book should rank for in their search engine. You can add **up to** 7 search keywords. Because each search keyword will increase your chances of ranking for that particular phrase, make sure you use up all seven, one per box.

Enter up to 7 search keywords that describe your book. How do I choose keywords? ▾

Your Keywords (Optional)

self-publishing	kindle books
publish paperback	publish a book on Amazon
publishing a book	kdp self publishing
createspace self publishing	

Again, **make sure you use all 7**. These keywords will make a big difference to your rankings on Amazon.

Categories

This section of the submission form allows you to choose the best categories for your book. Every category on Amazon has a best seller list just for that category. Therefore, it is possible to rank in the top 10 for any category you choose.

You can pick two categories.

Click on the **Set Categories** button to open up the category selection screen:

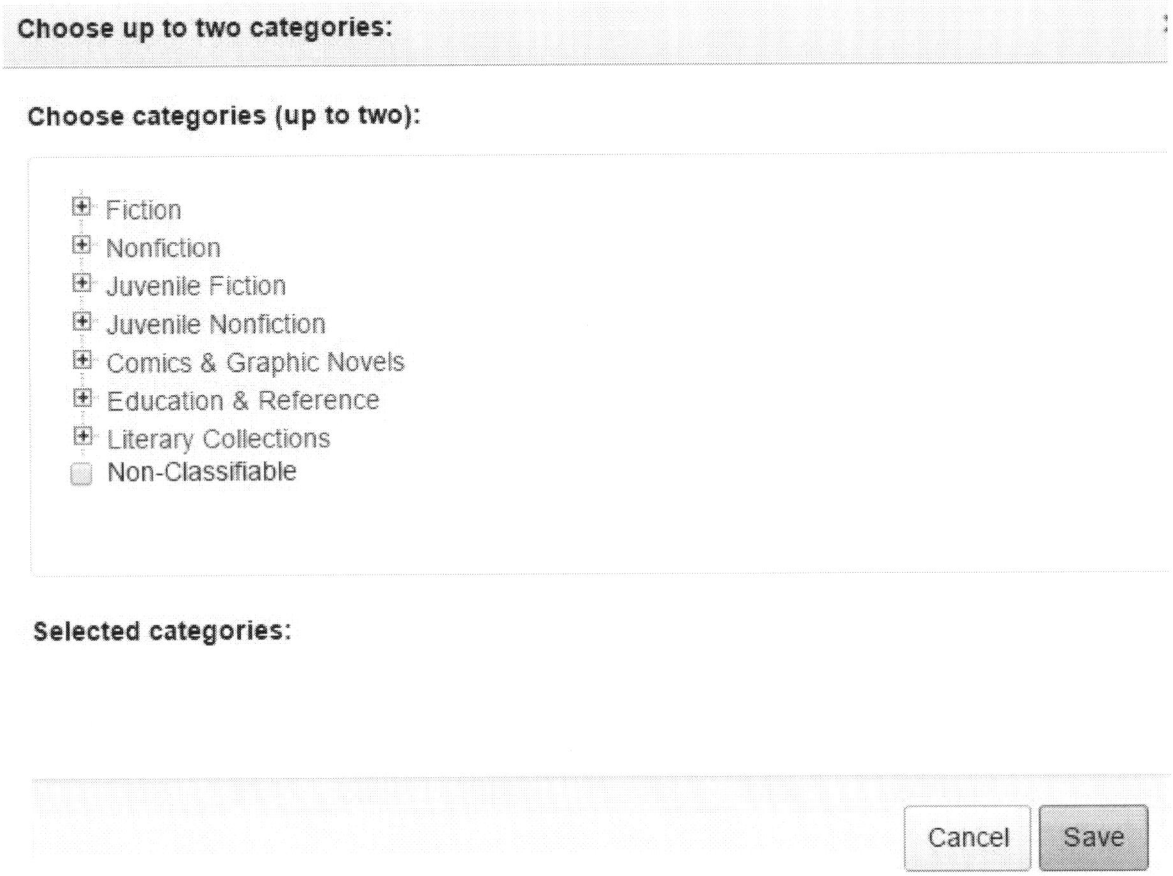

Choose up to two categories:

Choose categories (up to two):

- ⊞ Fiction
- ⊞ Nonfiction
- ⊞ Juvenile Fiction
- ⊞ Juvenile Nonfiction
- ⊞ Comics & Graphic Novels
- ⊞ Education & Reference
- ⊞ Literary Collections
- ☐ Non-Classifiable

Selected categories:

Cancel   Save

Most of the categories have sub-categories, so you need to expand the relevant section within the category tree, to find the two categories that best match your book. When you find the categories, check them off in the list and you'll see them added to the selected category list:

Choose categories (up to two):

- ☐ Political
- ☐ Psychological
- ☐ Religious
- ⊟ Romance
  - ☐ General
  - ☑ African American
  - ☐ Collections & Anthologies
  - ☐ Contemporary
  - ☐ Erotica
  - ☐ Fantasy
  - ☐ Gay

Selected categories:

Fiction > Romance > Historical > 20th Century Remove

Fiction > Romance > African American Remove

It is better to look for smaller sub-categories and not pick top level categories like "Romance. Top level categories will contain huge numbers of books making it much more difficult for your book to be seen in the category listings. Look for smaller sub-categories inside these top levels. Some sub-categories may have less than 10 books, so you'd be pretty much guaranteed of a top 10 listing in those categories.

There is something we've mentioned before that is probably very obvious to you now. The categories that Amazon displays on a product page, like these in the Best Sellers Rank section:

Amazon Best Sellers Rank: #14,485 Paid in Kindle Store (See Top 100 Paid in Kindle Store)
#7 in Kindle Store > Kindle eBooks > Nonfiction > Computers & Internet > **Web Site Design**
#12 in Books > Computers & Technology > Internet & Web Culture > **Blogging & Blogs**
#45 in Books > Computers & Technology > Web Development & Design > **Web Design**

.. do not correspond faithfully to the categories you will see when you come to submit your book.

For example, one of the categories above is:

Books > computers & technology > internet & web culture > blogging & blogs

If you search the category listings while you are submitting your book, you won't find a "Book" category. You also won't find a "Blogging & Blogs" category. This can make things a little more difficult as it means you'll have to go through ALL of the available categories to make sure you find the two most relevant. Choose the best two categories for your book.

TIP: If you want one of your books to appear in a particular category, but cannot find anything remotely similar in the Kindle category list, email the KDP support team and asked them what category to select so that the book appears in that category. The KDP help team are there to help YOU, so use them if you need any clarification.

Age and Grade Range

This is optional. If your book is intended for children, then you can select a minimum and maximum age and grade range. Amazon filters books according to these ranges, so if you want Amazon to suggest your book for a particular age or grade range, include that information in the submission form.

Pre-Order

With self-publishing, you have two options. You can publish it straight away, or you can schedule the publication of your book for as much as 90 days in the future. This allows you to collect pre-orders on your book which will be automatically delivered when it's published.

Be very careful about scheduling your book if it is not yet complete. Amazon does not like publishers that fail to meet their own deadline.

My advice is to start off by selecting the "I am ready to release my book now" option until you have a little more experience with KDP and understand how pre-orders may be used to your advantage. Be aware that the book won't actually be published until you finish filling out the submission forms, and click the "publish" button.

Once the information on this form is complete, click on the **Save and Continue** button at the bottom. If you want to just save it as a draft to come back to later, there is a button for that too.

If there are any errors or omissions on your form, you will get a notification like this:

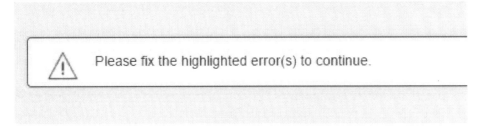

Fix the errors and continue to the "Kindle eBook Content" section of the form.

The first section of this form asks about Digital Rights Management (DRM):

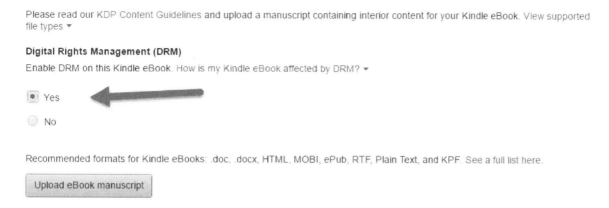

Check the radio button to enable digital rights management. Some people argue that you should not enable this, but I recommend you do. It makes it more difficult for people to illegally share your book. If you want to know why some people don't mind their books being distributed illegally, do a search on Google for "digital rights management".

You can now click the **Upload eBook Manuscript** button and upload the zip file you created earlier.

Once the upload is complete, you'll see a message like this:

It's now time to upload your eBook Cover.

If you have struggled with the cover, Amazon does offer a basic Cover Creator tool. If you want to check that out, click the button to launch the tool. It is beyond the scope of this book to show you how to use that, but it is relatively intuitive.

If you have a cover to upload, click the **Upload a cover you already have** radio button and the button to upload your cover will slide into place:

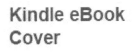
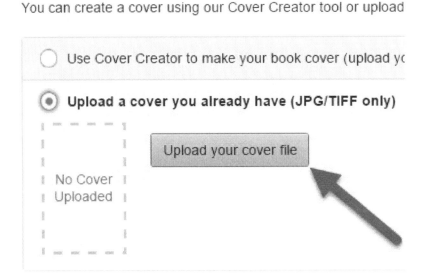

Click the upload button, and select it from your hard disk.

One successful completion, you'll see your cover in this area of the form:

Kindle eBook Preview

The next section of this form allows you to preview your book in the online previewer. It can take a little while to convert your book after the cover is uploaded, so be patient.

When ready, you might find that Amazon has added a warning about spelling mistakes in your book:

Click **View them** to open this web page:

— Back to Content

Possible spelling errors

To fix any of these potential spelling errors update your digital manuscript, then upload the corrected file. We also recommend running spell check if you have not done so.

1-4 of **4** possible spelling errors   Ignore all   Email to Me

Inisheer "Thank you for this book, Dr Andy!   Ignore

Minichester "Although I've already published several books on Kindle, there were plenty of great ideas here that I could take away and use.   Ignore

Mulenga "Another of Andy's well thought out and executed products.   Ignore

Rosana Hart "I was actually in the process of publishing a Kindle book when I opened this and I have to say it's filled out my knowledge in this area better than anything else I have seen or read.   Ignore

— Back to Content

As you can see, you can choose to ignore these spelling errors if they are not actually errors. If there are errors that need to be fixed in your book, go back to your Word document and correct them. Then re-save as web page filtered, zip it up and re-upload it.

Assuming you have fixed any errors, you can now click the **Launch Previewer** button to view your book as it will appear on Kindle devices.

Check your book, making sure images are all visible. Also check the formatting of the text, especially bullets and numbered lists. Go through the entire book to check it is perfectly formatted. When you are happy, you can close the previewer, and continue with the submission process.

Kindle eBook ISBN

This is optional as Kindle books do not require an ISBN.

If you want to use one, you can enter it here as well as the name of the publisher (also optional).

Unless you know you want an ISBN for your Kindle book, just leave these boxes empty and click the **Save and Continue** button to be taken to the Pricing screen.

KDP Select Enrollment

The first choice you have is whether or not to enroll your book into KDP Select for a 90-day period of exclusivity.

For the 90-day period that your book is in KDP, you cannot offer it for sale (or give it away for free), in any other digital format. Joining KDP means that you are making an exclusive agreement with Amazon.

KDP Select means that people can borrow your book for free if they are subscribers of Amazon Prime. For each borrow, you get a fee. The exact fee varies, but I don't want you to worry about this. The benefits of enrolling your book in KDP far outweigh any restrictions imposed on you. Amazon gives KDP Select authors a variety of powerful tools to help you promote your book. Therefore, I suggest you select the "Enroll" option.

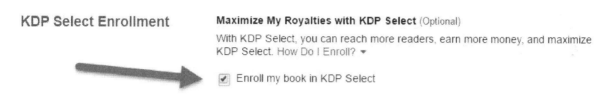

Territories

The next part of the submission form asks which territories you want your book sold in. Unless you have reason to exclude your book from specific territories, I recommend you select All Territories:

Rights & pricing

This section allows you to set the price of your book on the various Amazon stores, as well as "choose" your royalty rate.

Choose your royalty rate

KDP Pricing Support (Beta)
See the relationship between price and past sales and author earnings for KDP books like yours.

View Service

Select a royalty plan and set your Kindle eBook list prices below

○ 35%

◉ 70%

We talked about this earlier. We all want 70% royalty instead of 35%, so if your book is priced between $2.99 and $9.99, select the 70% option.

You can manually choose how much you want to charge for your book in each of the Amazon stores independently, but most people will want to charge the same equivalent value in all Amazon stores. Amazon makes this easy.

Enter the price you want in the US Amazon store. Amazon will work out the prices for the "Other Marketplaces".

If you want to sell your book at different "non-equivalent" prices on the various Amazon stores, you can do that too. Just edit the box for that country with the desired fee:

Amazon.es	€ 2.99 EUR	€2.47 without ES VAT	70%	€0.82	€1.16
	Must be €2.99-€9.99 ▼ Based on Amazon.com				
Amazon.it	€ 2.99 EUR	€2.45 without IT VAT	70%	€0.82	€1.14
	Must be €2.99-€9.99 ▼ Based on Amazon.com				
Amazon.nl	€ 2.99 EUR	€2.47 without NL VAT	70%	€0.82	€1.16
	Must be €2.99-€9.99 ▼ Based on Amazon.com				

Thoughts on pricing

Choosing a price for your book is not a simple task. A friend of mine wanted to publish his book on Kindle and told me that he wanted to sell his book for $16.99.

I asked him if his ultimate goal was to make as much money from book sales as possible, and he said that it was.

I took out my Smartphone and opened my calculator app. I explained that a Kindle book priced at $16.99 would only be eligible for 35% royalties, that's $5.95 per sale. If he sold his book for $9.99, he'd get 70% royalty, or $6.99 per sale. Not only would he make more profit at $9.99, but he'd probably also make more sales because the price was lower.

NOTE: A lower price is not always a better price.

In my testing, I offered one of my books at $0.99. When I increased the price to $2.99, the sales trebled. It's quite possible that if I increased the price to $4.99 the sales would increase again. Why? It's all to do with perceived value. People associate price with quality. Something that costs $0.99 is perceived as inferior by many people.

The only way you can find the best price for your books is to test different price points and see what happens to sales. I know this is probably not what you want to hear, but I can give you a tip.

Look at comparable books in your niche and find some that are written by largely unknown indie publishers. If you don't recognize the author's name, that's fine, just don't compare your book to Dean Koontz or Steven King novels. See how much other relatively unknown indie authors are charging for their book and do your best to price match it. That would be my starting point.

At a later date, you can start playing with the price to see if you can increase profits. Just remember that it is possible to increase your price, get FEWER sales, and yet still make more profit.

For example:

250 sales a month at $1.99 is $174 profit (remember that this one only qualifies for 35% royalty).

100 sales a month at $2.99 is $209 profit.

80 sales a month at $3.99 is $223 profit.

60 sales a month at $5.99 is $252 profit.

Matchbook

Kindle Matchbook is a promotional tool for KDP select authors. If you have a paperback version of your book, you can choose to offer your Kindle version to anyone that buys the paperback version. This offer can be a free copy or a nominal fee:

I always enroll my books in Matchbook and set the offer to "free".

Book Lending

Next on the submission page is a section on book lending. The check box for this should be grayed out since you chose the 70% royalty rate.

Book Lending

All books with 70% royalty rate are required to be enrolled in Kindle book lending.

Book lending means that people can lend your book to family and friends for a duration of 14 days. You can find out more about book lending by clicking the link in this section of the form.

At the bottom of the submission form is the **Terms & Conditions**.

By clicking the **Publish your Kindle eBook** button at the bottom of the form, you are agreeing to these terms and conditions.

When you are ready to publish your book, click the **Publish Your Kindle eBook** button.

That's it. Your book will take up to 48 hours to be published on Amazon (usually 12-24 hours for books written in English). Once your book is live, you'll be able to see it on Amazon and promote it using the strategies we discuss later in this book.

Updating your book

If you need to update your book description, categories, pricing, etc., just log into Kindle Direct Publishing again and you'll be taken to your Bookshelf. All of your published books will be listed there.

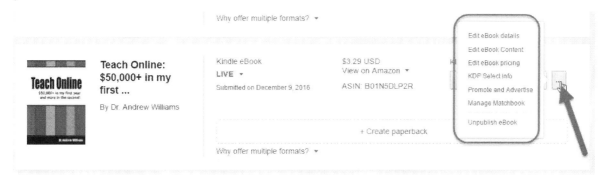

Next to each book is a button on the far right, that opens up a menu. This gives you access to edit all aspects of your book – details, content, pricing, etc.

Click the **Edit book details** link to go back to the submission form you filled in when you first submitted the book. The form will be populated with the currently saved data. Change whatever you want (upload a new version of the book, new cover image, change publication date, etc.), and then re-publish. The book will take time to update on Amazon, but the older version will continue to be available for purchase during the interim, so there is no "downtime" in terms of sales (unlike when you update a paperback).

If you want to change the pricing or territories, click the **Edit eBook Pricing** link in that menu. This takes you back to the same pricing & territories screen you saw before so that you can make the necessary changes. Again, it will take a few hours to update on Amazon, so until it does, your book will remain on sale at the original price and in the original territories.

Promoting your new Kindle book

Even though you probably don't realize it, we have actually done quite a lot to promote your book already:

1. The eye-catching cover

2. The high-quality book you've written

3. A great title

4. Choosing the best search keywords

5. Selecting appropriate categories that aren't too saturated with competition

6. Writing an enticing description that uses search keywords where possible.

Without the above in place, any further promotional strategies would pretty much fail in the long-term.

So, with a strong foundation built, what's next?

I'm sure you've read on the internet how you can and should promote your eBooks through social media channels like Facebook & Twitter. You may have even read a book by a best-selling Kindle author who advises you to use Twitter and/or a blog to promote you book(s). Well, I have tested social media and it really didn't work for me. In fact, talking with other self-publishers about this, social media really hasn't worked that well for any of them, UNLESS they had an established audience to begin with.

The biggest "secret" to promoting your book on Kindle is to:

1. Get a lot of downloads.

2. Get some good reviews & "Likes".

When you do this properly, Amazon actually takes over the promotion of your book, and if it's good, there is a great chance that it will take off. We'll look at methods of accomplishing these steps.

From what you have read so far, you may have the impression that I don't use social media in my Kindle promotional strategy. That's not entirely true. In fact, the first thing I recommend you do is set up a presence on Facebook and Twitter. However, this is not so you can blast out book promotions for your first book. It's so those who have read your book can contact and interact with you. Building a loyal fan base is an often over-looked aspect of marketing on Kindle, but loyal fans are far more than just people who will buy your future books. They are people who will help sell your books to their family & friends, to their Twitter followers or Facebook contacts. They are people who will ultimately defend you online when trolls come out of the woodwork and take a swipe at you or your work. Don't underestimate the power that even a small number of loyal fans can have on your own success. Make the effort to respond to people who contact you about your work, and make it personal. Talk to them as you would your friends.

In this section of the book, I want to bring the entire promotional strategy together. I'll also discuss a few strategies that you may have heard about from other Kindle authors (some are dangerous to your long-term success and should be avoided at all costs).

The goal of our promotion is simple. **We want to make Amazon sit up and take notice of our book.** Once they do, they'll start promoting the book for you. When that happens, sales can really take off.

Here is a bird's eye view of the strategy we are going to use. You should bear in mind that these things work together so that the sum of the whole is greater than the sum of the individual parts. You should complete all of the steps, but don't worry, I'll show you how.

1. You have a high-quality book with an effective cover, title, and description. It should have well-chosen search keywords and 2 relevant categories that are not too competitive (we want to be able to get into the top 10 for our chosen categories, eventually).

2. You have a Facebook page in your author name so as to keep in contact with readers and bond with them. You can also have a blog if you want one, though a Facebook page is more important early on because of the way status updates on your page will be seen on other Facebook user pages, thus extending your visibility. "Fans" who post on your Facebook page are naturally spreading the word about you and your books to THIER Facebook "fans". That's how Facebook works and why social channels become very powerful

3. You set up a Twitter account in your author name so people can follow you and keep up-to-date with your releases. This is also a second channel of contact between you and your readers.

4. You set up an Author Central profile. This is a page on Amazon about you, the author. It links to your Facebook page and Twitter profile so readers can easily find a way to contact you.

5. You set up a free promotion on Amazon to get as many downloads as possible. During the promotion, you need to "advertise" your promotion around the web. Hopefully, this will lead to your book getting reviews and "Likes".

6. Once reviews come in, you need to use the "Look Inside" feature of your book to further pre-sell your title.

7. To sell more books, write more books. You should think about serializing your work or creating a "series" where books all target the same audience. This can be done in fiction and non-fiction, and will really help sales of all books in the series because, with more books, there is a higher chance your books will be discovered.

We'll go through each of these steps in turn so that you can set this up. We'll also discuss how each of these steps helps in the overall promotion of your book.

Setting up a Gmail account

It's always a good idea to separate your book publishing from your private life, so the first thing we are going to do is set up a Gmail account in your author name. You'll use this exclusively for all matters related to your author name/books. If you eventually publish more books under a different pen name, you should create a new Gmail account for each pen name.

Head on over to Google and search for Gmail. You'll find it listed #1 in Google. Click through to the Gmail website.

Already own a Gmail account?

You may already have a Gmail account or two, but the one we are creating now is only to be used for stuff relating to your books.

If you have other Gmail accounts, Google will ask you to log in with one of them. There is no obvious place to click to create a new account. In this case, click on **Use Another Account**.

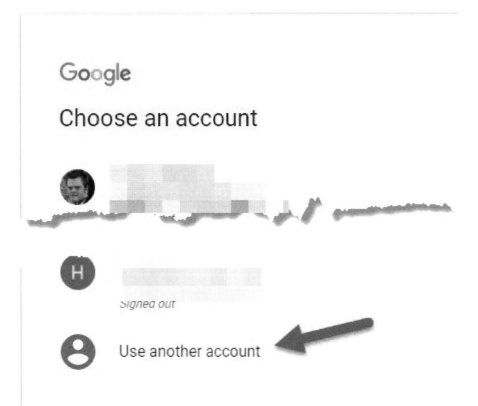

On the next screen, click **More Options** and select **Create Account**. You'll then be taken to the form to create your new Gmail.

Your first Gmail account?

If this is your first Gmail account, you will see a button to create an account. Click it and go through the process of filling in the form to set up your new Gmail.

You'll be asked to enter a first name, last name and so on. An important field is the username. You want your author name included here but chances are it will already be taken. If that is the case, you can add the word "author" after your name, as that is far more likely to be available. e.g. if susandoyle@Gmail.com is taken, try susandoyleauthor@Gmail.com.

Use this email address for everything related to your books.

Step 1 – High-quality book & cover

Already in this book, we have discussed the importance of the book cover, the title, and the description. These all appear on your book product page and can make the difference between sales and no sales.

These aspects of your book have to look as professional as possible. Also, don't forget that your book needs to be high quality. If your book is bad, you'll get bad reviews. Negative reviews kill sales, so make your book the best it can be. That way, when the rest of the promotion engine gets going, you'll get sales, which leads to good reviews, which leads to increased sales, which leads to Amazon taking notice. At that point, they'll start promoting your book for you.

Related to this, you chose 2 categories that were relevant to your book and made sure they weren't too competitive (you stayed out of the top-level categories). You also made use of your 7 allocated search keywords. Your product page is now set up and optimized as well as it can be in order to rank in the Amazon search engine, and so promote sales of your book.

Step 2 – Facebook page

We have talked about the importance of having loyal fans. To get loyal fans, there has to be a way for them to contact you. You do have your new Gmail address but they are unlikely to know that in the beginning. You should set up a Facebook page in your author's name. We'll look at how to do that in a moment.

I'd also suggest that when you have time, you set up a blog in your author's name. Blogs can be set up for free on platforms like blogger.com or wordpress.com, but these blogs do have a number of limitations. I'd, therefore, recommend that when you're able to, you buy your own domain and set up a WordPress blog on that. Teaching you how to set up a WordPress blog is beyond the scope of this book, but I have other books and courses that you can use if you want to learn. Check out the resources section at the end of this book for details.

When you are just starting out, the Facebook page is far more important than the blog, so for now, let's just set up the Facebook page. I'll assume you already have a personal Facebook account (if not, you should sign up for one).

Setting up a Facebook page

It's not a great idea to mix business and pleasure on Facebook. Liking and commenting on your granny's apple pie photo one minute, then promoting your new thriller the next, is not a great way to run your publishing business. People interested in your books are not interested in your granny, unless, of course, they are family members.

The way we get around this is to set up a Facebook Page (not to be confused with your Facebook personal profile). These are totally separate from your personal timeline.

Whatever you post on a Facebook page does not get posted on your personal timeline. You can, therefore, keep business and everyday life completely separate.

Think of a Facebook page as a business listing where people can find out details of your business – in this case, you the author. You need to come up with a suitable name for your Facebook page.

Start off with your author name, exactly as it appears on your book covers. If your cover shows your book was written by John P. Smith, then that should be what you are looking to use on your Facebook page. You want people to easily find you.

If that is taken, then you could use something like John P. Smith Author, John P. Smith Publishing, etc.

By doing this, people searching for you as an author on Facebook would easily spot your page in the search results.

If you are writing a series of books called "Out of Nowhere", you could call your Facebook page "Out of Nowhere". This would make it easy for fans of the series to find your Facebook page in Google.

Facebook & Pennames

For those publishing under a pen name, you may be wondering whether you can just set up a new Facebook personal profile in the author's pen name. In many ways this would be easier, BUT, Facebook is clamping down on "fake" accounts. No single person should have more than one Facebook account – those are Facebook's rules.

You could argue that you and your persona are two separate people and therefore it's OK. It's a fine line and only you can make that decision. Personally, I like to make sure that what I do today does not cause me problems further down the line, so I prefer the idea of a Facebook page. Think of these as "business" sections of your Facebook account. You can set up a Facebook page for anything – your favorite band, your website or your pet cat. You can set up a Facebook page for each of your pen names, or each of the book series you write. Facebook pages are an easy way to have a business listing on the web without having to pay for your own website.

Okay, let's set up the Facebook Page.

I'll assume you have a personal Facebook account already. If not, you'll need to sign up for one. Once you have done that, log in and we can get started.

When you log in, click on the **Home** link in the top menu. You should then find a link to create a Page at the bottom of the left sidebar.

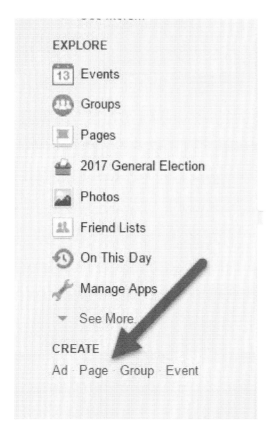

Click it.

The "Create a Page" screen has several options.

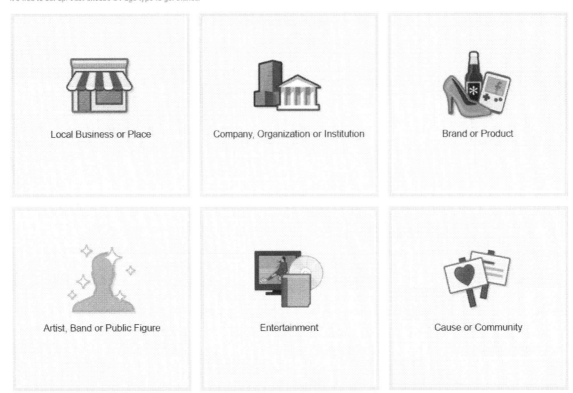

The one you want to choose is "Artist, Band or Public Figure".

There is an Author option in the drop-down list. Type your author name underneath and click the **Get Started** button.

You will be taken to your author Facebook Page with a number of options to complete:

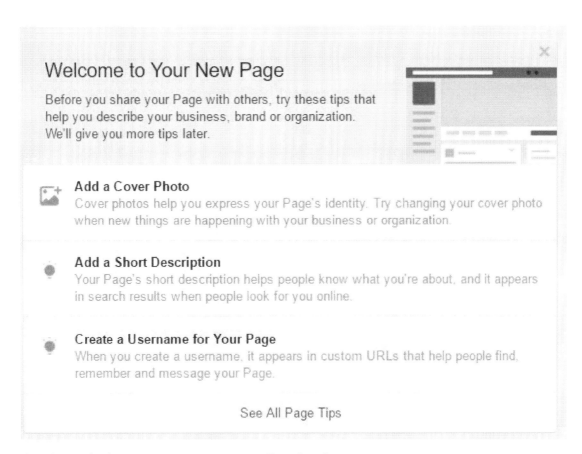

Welcome to Your New Page

Before you share your Page with others, try these tips that help you describe your business, brand or organization. We'll give you more tips later.

Add a Cover Photo
Cover photos help you express your Page's identity. Try changing your cover photo when new things are happening with your business or organization.

Add a Short Description
Your Page's short description helps people know what you're about, and it appears in search results when people look for you online.

Create a Username for Your Page
When you create a username, it appears in custom URLs that help people find, remember and message your Page.

See All Page Tips

Go through the steps to setup your Facebook page.

1. Add a cover photo.

2. Add a short description.

3. Create a username for your page.

Facebook offers help with these steps, so go ahead and complete your page before moving on.

From now on, when you log into your personal Facebook account and click on your home tab, your Facebook page(s) will appear in the left sidebar.

Clicking the link to your Facebook page will open it.

At the top of your newly created Facebook page, you'll see a menu that gives you access to your page settings.

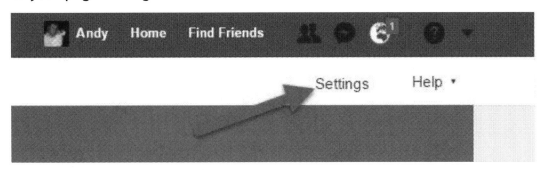

There are a huge number of settings you can change, so we won't be going through them here. It is worth exploring these to familiarize yourself with your new Facebook page. Pay particular attention to the General tab of settings, as these control a number of publishing and privacy settings.

You can write status updates on your Facebook page in exactly the same way as you do on your normal, personal Facebook account. You should use status updates to talk about your books or to mention when new releases are coming up, and the timing of any free promotions (see later). If you are a non-fiction writer, you can also use it for posting "industry" news.

Step 3 – Twitter account

Your Twitter account will be used mainly to update followers on the release dates and free promos of future books. Some people will tell you that it is also a great way to get new customers for your books, but I haven't found that myself. I see Twitter as part of my long-term marketing plan as well as a channel through which my "fans" can stay in touch.

Some of your readers will probably contact you through Twitter with direct messages, so always try to respond to them in a timely and professional manner. Remember that we are trying to build a loyal following that will buy, promote, and defend our work for us. Every single person who contacts you is important to your future success, so be nice, and talk to them as you would your friends.

Incidentally, you should always be polite, even to rude people, no matter how hard it is.

Setting up a Twitter account for your author name

To sign up for Twitter in your author's name, go to twitter.com and click the **Sign up** button.

Join Twitter today.

| John P. Smith | ✓ |

| johnpsmithauthor@gmail.com | ✓ |

| •••••••••••• | ✓ |

Sign up

By signing up, you agree to the Terms of Service and Privacy Policy, including Cookie Use. Others will be able to find you by email or phone number when provided.

Advanced options

Fill in your full name, Gmail address and a password and click the **Sign up** button.

You'll be taken to a screen that asks for your phone number which is supposed to make your account more secure. Be aware you can skip this step. Look for the small **Skip** link.

On the next screen, you get to choose your Twitter username.

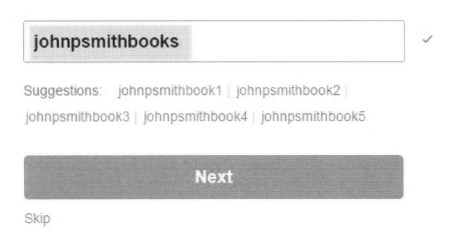

There is a character limit of 15 characters, so in the example above, I could not use johnpsmithauthor and plain old johnpsmith was already taken.

You can change this later, so don't worry too much if you cannot think of the best username to use right now. Just enter a working username and click **Next**.

You will be asked a series of questions to get your Twitter account started, so just go through the steps until you get to your **Welcome Home** screen. That's it, you now have a Twitter account for use with your publishing empire.

Twitter will have sent you a confirmation email, so find it, and click the link to confirm your new account.

I would recommend you now fill in your profile, add a photo, etc. You can access all the settings by clicking the image in the menu at the top:

When the setup process is complete, you'll have a Twitter account in the name of your author, with photo, short bio, etc..

If you go to the **settings and privacy** settings, then click on the **Apps** menu, you can link your Twitter and Facebook accounts. By doing this, you can post your tweets to Facebook automatically.

If you set up a blog...

.. and I should say that this is totally optional at this stage, but if you do decide on a blog, make sure comments are enabled but require moderation to appear. Also make sure you have links (icons are better than text links), to your Twitter account and Facebook page so that people arriving at your blog have additional ways to get in touch with you. I'd recommend adding a Facebook and Twitter "button" to your sidebar and have these images link to your Facebook Page and Twitter Profile.

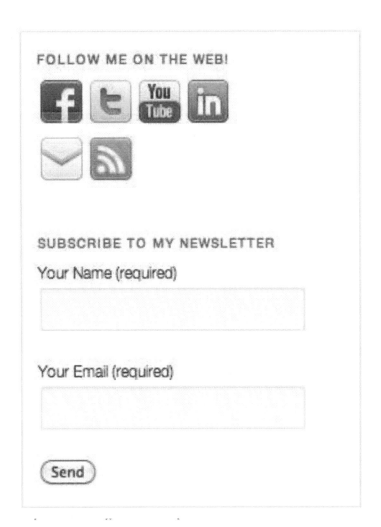

NOTE: You can also have a newsletter subscription form on the sidebar if you want to start collecting subscribers (that you can sell your books to). This requires a separate autoresponder/newsletter service like Aweber, and setting this up is beyond the scope of this book. If you want to sign up for a free trial at Aweber, go to **ezseo.aweber.com** and click the free trial button in the top menu.

Step 4 – Author Central

As soon as your book is published in the Kindle Marketplace, you should set up your author profile in Author Central. Think of this author page as a self-promotion page on Amazon. There will be a biography as well as other information and a link to all your books.

NOTE: There are actually several Author Central sites catering for authors in different countries. For English language books, the one in the US and one in the UK are important and you should set up both. I'll show you the process for the US site and you can just repeat the steps for the UK. However, please note that not all of the features found in the US Author Central are available in the others.

Go over to Author Central:

US: http://authorcentral.amazon.com/

UK: https://authorcentral.amazon.co.uk

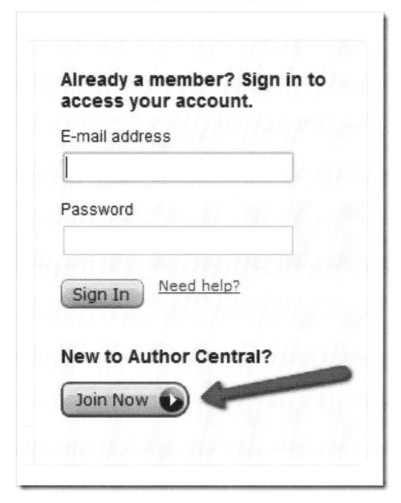

Click on the "Join Now" button, and then...

.. fill in your Amazon account username and password to log in. This is the same login you use when you buy stuff on Amazon.

You'll have to accept the terms they display.

The next screen asks you to enter your author name. Enter the same name you used during the book submission.

Please help us find and identify your books in the Amazon.com catalog.

What is your author name?

My author name is Andy Williams, Ph.D.

Continue ▶

Click the **Continue** button.

Amazon will then show you a list of books. If you see your book you can select it to add to your Author Central profile.

If you don't see your book, click the link at the bottom "I am someone else", and you can enter more search details, like the book title or even the ASIN (Amazon Standard Identification Number). Amazon will try again to find your book. When you find your book, select it to add to your profile.

Once you are set up with Author Central, Amazon will send you a confirmation email. You will then need to click on the verification link in that email to activate your profile.

Once confirmed, go to Author Central and log in. Click the link to **Author Page** in the top menu:

You will be taken to a blank author profile, ready for you to edit. Click the edit biography link and enter a short biography. This can be changed later, so don't worry too much about getting it perfect.

Edit biography

close ⊠

Please follow the below guidelines to ensure your submission is acceptable:

- Include a minimum of 100 characters (about 20 words)
- Use plain text only - no rich formatting (bolds, italics) or HTML
- Be creative: share anecdotes or interesting details about yourself with your readers
- See a sample biography .

After graduating from Hull University (North Humberside, UK), I went on to do a Ph.D. at Cardiff University where I studied endocrinology in fish. After working as a research associate at Cardiff University I decided I wanted to be a teacher, so went back to University (this time Birmingham) to study for a teaching certificate.

My first teaching job took me to Tenerife, Spain where I met my wife to be. After a spell of teaching in Madrid, we went back to Tenerife. Two kids later, we now live in North Wales.

ON a day to day basis, I write how to books and courses related to websites, SEO and other topics of interest to anyone running a website.

Preview biography ▶

NOTE: the biography is text based, so you cannot include HTML or formatting.

Within Author Central, you can add the RSS feed of your website if you have one.

If you have a Wordpress website, then the URL of the feed will be your domain name, with **/feed** appended to the end.

This will then display the contents of your RSS feed on your author page.   Here it is on my author profile:

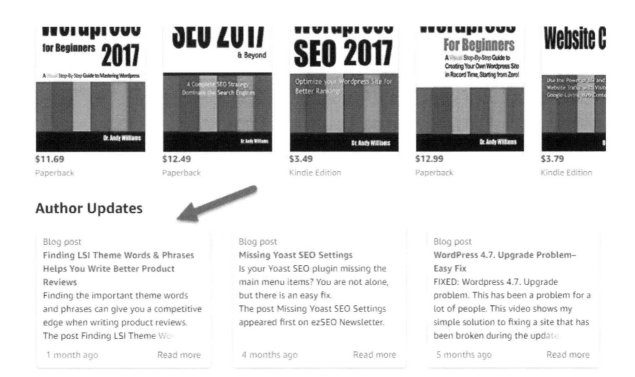

This is really useful because any posts you publish on your "author website", will show up on your Amazon author profile.

To add a feed, click the **add blog** link:

The **Add an RSS feed** screen appears:

Add an RSS feed   close ⊠

Author Central supports all versions of RSS and Atom blog feeds. Posts created before you add this feed will not be imported. If you want previous posts to appear on the Author Page, please re-post them on your home blog.

Example RSS feed URLs:

- http://www.omnivoracious.com/atom.xml
- http://www.aldenteblog.com/rss.xml
- http://www.chordstrike.com/index.rdf

Specify an RSS feed for your blog

Add your Feed URL and then click the **Add** button.

Your feed will appear in the **Blog feed** section:

Next, add a photo to your profile:

Choose a good photograph of yourself, or your persona (you can use images from photo sites if you want to remain anonymous).

Author page URL

One other thing you can do while you are here is to create an author profile page URL. Choose a URL that is easy to remember and includes your author name, like you did for your Facebook page. In fact, you could use the exact same name on both the Amazon profile and Facebook page. The easier it is for people to identify these pages as belonging to you, the better.

You can see that I have added mine here:

You need to pick a unique URL, so you may have to play around with it to find one that is accepted. Once you have done this, it will take 30 minutes or so to get that URL working. Once it is, share your author page on your Twitter and Facebook channels using the neat URL you just created.

OK, we are finished. You can now view your profile page either by clicking the link at the top of the current screen:

.. or by going to your newly created author profile page using the URL you just setup.

Here is mine:

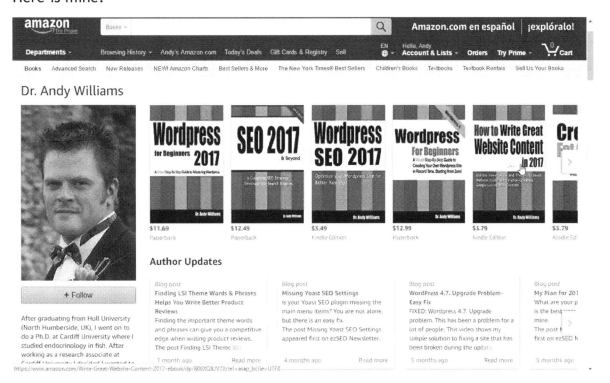

You can see my biography underneath the photo with a list of my books to the right. Under these, you can see my most recent blog posts (taken from my website RSS feed).

OK; now you need to go and create your author profile on Author Central UK.

https://authorcentral.amazon.co.uk

You can use the exact same information entered into your US profile.

Adding new books to your author profile

Any time you release a new book, you may need to manually add it to your Author Central accounts.

To do this, log into Author Central and click the link to **Books** in the menu bar at the top:

Click the **Add more books** button:

You'll get a search box that allows you to search for your book(s). Under each book in the results list is a button labeled "This is my book". Click the button under your book.

As long as everything is OK, and it is confirmed that the book is yours, it will be added to your Author Central profile within a few days.

Step 5 – Get downloads, reviews & likes on Amazon

Getting a lot of downloads is the secret to kickstart book sales. What I am about to tell you might go against what your gut tells you, but bear with me.

OK, here goes...

I want you to offer your book for FREE for 5 full days, one after another.

Why 5 full days?

Because that is what Amazon gives you. When you enroll your book in KDP Select, you are essentially becoming exclusive to Amazon for the next 90 days. In return, Amazon allows you to give your book away for free, for 5 days within the 90.

OK, so why do we want to give it away for free? I thought the idea was to make money on our books?

Well, it is, but when a book is free, it will get a lot of downloads.

So?

The more "free downloads" your book gets, the more exposure it has.   And the more exposure your book gets, the more likely you are to get feedback in the form of reviews on Amazon, messages on Facebook, Twitter, etc. from people that have read it.

Lots of downloads are one of the secret ingredients to a successful book launch on Kindle. Getting reviews is the other. Get these two things and your book has a great chance of catching Amazon's "eye". This is when their own promotional engine takes over.

Sounds easy, doesn't it? Well, the sad truth is that many people who download your book are unlikely to read it, let alone leave a review. This really is a numbers game. What we need to do is publicize the fact the book will be free, and secondly, ASK for the review.

If you are established in your niche, then you may already have a mailing list that you can use to promote your free download period. If you are just starting out, then you need to find other places where you can promote the book and get it downloaded and hopefully reviewed.

Fortunately, there are a number of websites that will publicize your freebie to their audience, many for free.   Some of these sites will want advanced notice of the promotion dates, while others will only want to be notified when the book is actually available.

Besides relying on the freebie downloaders, where else can you get reviews?

Friends & family are one option. If you are active on any social media (Facebook, Twitter, Google+, Pinterest, etc.) then that is another option. While I am sure that Amazon doesn't like this type of "friend" review, we do all need a little leg-up when first starting out, so just don't make it too obvious.   I recommend you only ask people to leave a review IF they read your book AND they like it.

Consider sending review copies to people that might be interested in your book. Ask them to include a sentence in their review stating that they received a review copy. That will keep Amazon happy.

Ask everyone you know to:

1. Write an objective review and not just "Great book" with 5 stars. If they think the book deserves a 5 star, then great, but don't forget that a 4 star is still a great score! At this point, getting four or five good reviews is critical.

2. If they enjoyed the book, ask them to mention it to their friends, tweet it on Twitter, and/or post on Facebook, etc.

Setting up the Free Promotion in Amazon

I'll explain the full promotion schedule in a moment, but first, let me show you how to set up the free promotion in Amazon.

1. Log into KDP.

2. On the Bookshelf tab, click the **Promote and Advertise** button next to the book you want to promote.

The screen that loads will show your KDP Select status at the top. It will tell you when you enrolled in KDP and when your 90-day exclusivity period finishes. If you decide you want to take your book out of KDP, you can click the **Manage KDP Select Enrollment** button and uncheck the box to automatically renew it into the KDP Select program.

You will see a section on this page called **Run a Price Promotion**.

Run a Price Promotion

Sign your book up for a Kindle Countdown Deal or a Free Book Promotion. Only one promotion can be enabled per enrollment period.

○ Kindle Countdown Deal Learn more
◉ Free Book Promotion Learn more

Create a new Free Book Promotion

Select **Free Book Promotion** and click the **Create a new Free Book Promotion** button.

The screen that opens allows you to choose a starting date and end date.

A lot of sites where you can promote your free book giveaway require a little notice, often 5 – 7 days. Therefore, if you intend to notify any websites about your giveaway, it is best to schedule your giveaway for a week into the future to give yourself time.

Enter your start and end date and click the **Save Changes** button. You will now see your promotion has been setup:

Promotions & Advertisements for this book

All ⋄

Benefit Type	Marketplace	Start	End	Status	
Kindle Countdown Deal	Amazon.com	August 25, 2016	August 31, 2016	Complete	
Kindle Countdown Deal	Amazon.co.uk	August 25, 2016	August 31, 2016	Complete	
Free Book Promotion		June 14, 2017	June 15, 2017	Scheduled	› Edit ⟩ Delete

Notice that you can edit or delete the promotion if you change your mind, but don't leave it until the last minute.

OK, now we know how to set up a free promotion, let's look at the promotion schedule.

Free promotion schedule

Here are the steps for scheduling the free promotion:

1. Choose a date for your promotion. I personally include a weekend within the 5 days of my promotion, as weekends have performed better for me than weekdays. However, I have heard other people say the opposite. You may need to test this yourself to find the best days for your own promotions, as I am sure it may depend on the type of book. Personally, I'd start a free promotion on a Thursday or Friday and leave it running for 5 days straight. Set up the free promotion on Amazon.

2. **At least 7 days before the promotion:** If you already have your book published, and therefore know the Amazon URL or ASIN number, submit your book to the free promotional sites that require several days' notice. You'll know the dates of your free promotion.

3. On **day one** of your promotion, contact the free promotional sites that only accept submissions for books that are currently free. Submit your book to these sites.

4. Leave the promo running. After the 5 days are up, your book will automatically revert to the paid version on Amazon.

At any time during this process, you can get some reviews. As soon as you get a couple of positive reviews for your book, move onto the "Look Inside" Feature (below).

Lists of sites that can promote your book

There are a lot of websites out there that allow you to submit your book when it is on a free promotion. These sites then promote your book to their own visitors, so your book can potentially get a lot of exposure.

The list of websites promoting free book giveaways is constantly changing (some disappearing, new ones appearing). Therefore, I have published it on my website for convenience. You can find that list here:

https://goo.gl/w3t9mW

Remember, some of these sites require notice; others require that your book is free at the time of submission (the web page above does differentiate between these two types of submission site), so bear that in mind as you schedule your promotion.

Kindle Countdown Deals

Amazon also allows KDP Select books to use **Kindle Countdown Deals**. The idea here is to allow publishers to offer their books at a discount for a limited time, with a visible countdown timer.

Whether this is something you want to use, probably depends on your own situation. For example, this is something I would use (instead of a free promotion) when book sales started to decrease. It is also something I would use if I released a major update on my book, just to bring it back into the attention of potential buyers.

The advantages of the Kindle Countdown include:

1. You can control how long your book is on special offer and those visiting your book sales page will see the time remaining for the special offer pricing before it returns to its normal price.

2. You can offer your book below $2.99 during a Kindle Countdown, and still qualify for 70% commission if your book normally gets 70% commission.

3. Amazon has a Kindle Countdown Deals page (www.amazon.com/Kindlecountdowndeals) where offers are shown. While you will be competing against a lot of other people for a slot at the top, this chart will offer extra exposure for your book.

4. KDP has a report to monitor sales and royalties in real-time at each price, discounted or pre-promotion, to help you monitor your results.

In reality, I have never found Kindle Countdown deals to be very effective. That might just be my own books, so you might want to test this for yourself.

Step 6 - The "Look Inside" feature

As soon as you have received a couple of good reviews for your book, work on the "Look Inside" feature. When I added this feature to my first Kindle eBook, sales increased between 50-70%! Since then, I've added it to all of my books ASAP.

So, what is this feature?

For Kindle books, Amazon has a "Look Inside" feature that allows visitors to the Amazon website to look inside the book. Needless to say, this helps people to decide whether they want to buy it or not.

Visitors on Amazon can simply click the book cover to see inside.

Amazon will show the first 10% of the book's content. Knowing that, we can use it to our advantage to help promote the book.

Go through the comments that people have left for your book, and pull out any quotes that praise you or your book. Get as many as you can (and don't forget to add more as you get additional reviews in the future).

Now, create a section at the start of your book (I recommend adding it before the table of contents if you have one):

What people are saying about this book:

"I work in the education department at one of the top academic institutions in the U.S. and if I could hire Dr. Williams to write all of my online training, I wouldn't hesitate..." **Laurie**

"Wow! From someone who is not a beginner to Wordpress." **Albert J**

"Definitely the go-to guide! Since Wordpress is a pretty easy format to get started on, I was able to make some progress. Then I found Wordpress for Beginners and WOW - my progress took off. Having a visual guide with

Over time, add all of the positive comments that people are saying about you or your book, and make sure you include the name of the reviewer.

If you are a fiction writer and have several books on sale, you could create a "What people are saying about John Blackstone" section instead. This would be different in that the comments are about you, the author, and not about that particular book. The advantage here is that you have a readymade "What people are saying..." section for any new book you release without having to wait for reviews on the new book itself. This is what John Locke does.

I'd also include links to your Facebook and Twitter pages within the first 10% of your book. If you have a blog set up, add that as well. By doing this, even if someone decides not to buy the book, they still know where they can contact or follow you.

A note for fiction writers

You'll probably want to make sure that enough of your story is found in the first 10% so that potential customers will be able to read enough of the book to get them hooked. I'd also make sure there is a "What people are saying.." section, but, this will be a balancing act between how much story and how many testimonials are included in the Look Inside feature.

For non-fiction writers, I personally don't worry too much about how much of the book content is included in the first 10%. As long as you include a "What people are saying section" and a table of contents, then people know what they are getting.

OK, that's the main promotional strategy for your first book. However, as you move forward as an author, there is one thing you can do to sell more books. Write more books! This is where we should discuss serialization, which is extremely powerful for boosting sales.

Step 7 - Serialization of your books

What do I mean by serialization? Well, it's a number of related books, sold as a series. For example, I could set up a "Webmaster Series" of books and include my SEO book, WordPress book, and CSS book. They are all related and therefore might be of interest to someone who bought one of the other two.

For fiction writers, it's a similar concept. It's a set of books that are related to one another. This relationship might be:

1. One book follows on from another so that the "whole" story is split up into separate books. We'll see the same main characters appear in each book (unless they are killed off!). A good example of this is the Harry Potter series.

2. The main character flows through all the books, but individual stories are not related to each other. An example here could be John Locke's Donovan Creed series. Each book in that series is a completely separate story, but the main character is one and the same.

So why create a series?

Well, there are a number of reasons:

1. People who like one book in the series are likely to buy the next. If your series is good, you'll build up a loyal fan base, which, as we mentioned earlier, is one of our main goals as indie publishers.

2. You can give away the first book in a series to get readers hooked on the story. If they like it, they'll buy the other books in that series. The more books they read, the more likely they'll become a loyal fan and a paying customer of your other works.

3. Each book in a series, where the story is continued from one to the next, will leave the reader wanting to buy the next one to find out what happens.

4. The more books you have out there, the more likely it is that someone will find your work and become a paying customer.

5. You can package up a series into a larger product and sell it at a discounted price when compared to the cost of buying each book in the series individually. Faced with saving money, many people will buy the series "bundle" saving themselves a few bucks in the process. Many people who do buy the bundle would not have bought all the books in the series anyway. The other good thing about bundles is that they build fan loyalty because your buyers get to see that you offer more value for money.

A popular trend over the last couple of years is for new indie publishers to write a book and split it into three parts, releasing it as three separate "novellas". The first book ends on a cliff-hanger, encouraging the reader to buy the second one and so on.

These "novellas" are priced at the lower range, so readers don't mind this. However, where many indie publishers go wrong is that they release part 1 and wait to see what sales are like. They will eventually see sales die off and this kills motivation. Chances are they'll decide that it's not worth spending the time and effort to write part 2 or part 3. This leaves readers feeling cheated. This scenario is actually quite common.

Compare that to what might happen if you wrote all three parts before releasing the first one.

When someone finishes the first book, the second one is available. When they finish that one, the next is available. Anyone who gets to the end of the third book is likely to be a loyal fan by then, and that means they are now part of your promotional army – buying, promoting (telling friends & family) and defending your reputation against trolls. That's a completely different type of reader to the first scenario.

In 2012, when I was looking for inspiration to start publishing on Kindle, I read a novella by a fellow Internet Marketer. Let's call it book 1, series 1, as the author planned it as a 3-part story. I read the book in an afternoon and really enjoyed it. I would have bought the second book if it had been available, but it wasn't. In fact, the second book never materialized. If she ever does release parts 2 and 3, I won't be buying them. She lost me as a reader.

Think what this has done to her reputation as a writer. Maybe she gets a new idea for a series (let's call this series 2) and is so excited by the idea that she writes book 1 in series 2, before completing series 1. How many people who bought book 1 of series 1 would buy book 1 of series 2? Probably not very many because they wouldn't have much faith that the story would ever get finished.

I can see why this author lost interest in her project. From her point of view, she would have seen a good spike in sales with her Amazon Best Seller's Rank hitting the top 5,000 or higher for a while. She *was* making good daily sales. However, as the weeks passed by, the Seller's Rank dropped, meaning she wasn't making daily sales. What motivation did she now have to continue with that story?

Had she written all three books in the series and released them shortly after one another, sales of each novella would have helped drive the sales of the others. She could also move onto a new project knowing she had fans that would probably buy & promote her next book, and defend her reputation.

Whatever type of books you write, consider the added benefits of writing serialized books. This really is one of the more powerful marketing strategies, especially for the fiction writer. Just be clever with it. If you plan a 3-book series, don't release book 1 before book 2 is complete, or at least nearly finished. And make sure book 3 is ready to be released soon afterward. As I mentioned earlier, an ideal situation would be to have all three books ready (or at least first draft), BEFORE releasing the first one.

What not to do when promoting your book

I have read a number of blog posts and books on Kindle publishing. Some give good advice, whereas others offer VERY bad advice. You need to remember that Kindle is Amazon's business. If Amazon thinks you are abusing its system, it can and will shut you down. Are you prepared to take that risk?

I thought not.

Here is a list of things I strongly advise you NOT to do.

1. **Do not buy reviews**. Bestselling Kindle author John Locke has admitted to buying reviews. You can read the full story on https://goo.gl/DFyxd. Some people think that buying reviews is no worse than giving your book away and asking for a review. The reviewer is getting something in return for their review. I personally don't see a problem with asking people to review your book IF they like it, even though it was a free download. However, paying people to leave reviews is clearly not what Amazon wants for its review system. That also goes for paying people to leave bad reviews on your competitor's products. It does happen, but my advice to you is DON'T do it.

2. **Do not create fake Amazon accounts** and leave reviews yourself. I have seen this many times and it's usually quite obvious. Lots of reviewers, usually without photos, only ever reviewing the one product, or a range (or series), of products by the same author.

3. **Do not hijack other people's product pages** with reviews that have links to your own book. This is another tactic that I have read about and it's a tactic that one author teaches in his popular Kindle book. Again, this is a clear tactic to try and manipulate the rankings system. Amazon is deleting reviews that they think are bogus, and this type of review screams fake. Don't get other people to leave this type of review either.

Although a few years old, this article is worth a read: https://goo.gl/eFSHD

How Facebook page & Twitter fit into your promotional strategy

Your Twitter and Facebook accounts will become more valuable to you as you become better known for your books. You'll be able to use those accounts (and that blog you'll eventually set up), to announce free promo days and any new books. However, don't think that these accounts are something you should leave until "later". Set them up NOW, because people who read your first book can and will contact you through Twitter and Facebook.

Teaching you how to use Facebook and Twitter is beyond the scope of this book, but there are some great free tutorials online that can help you out. Do a YouTube search for help.

Using YouTube to promote your books

If you have the skills required to create videos for YouTube, then you have an advantage. YouTube can give you a lot of free exposure.

Since YouTube is owned by Google, videos tend to rank really well on the Google search engine. If you are a fiction writer, you'll need to think creatively about how you could use YouTube to promote your books. Non-fiction writers have it a little easier, as you can just create small tutorials that then link to your book.

In your YouTube video description, you can include a link to your book.

Setting up tracking links

It's interesting to know whether links under your videos are being clicked. This isn't only valuable for links you place in YouTube video descriptions. If you write an article, submit it to another site and include a link to your book in the article, wouldn't it be nice to know how much traffic that link is sending you? If you know a particular site is a good source of traffic, you can use that site more often.

I'll show you how to set up this type of tracking on a WordPress site since most of you will eventually have one under your author's name.

Login to your WordPress dashboard.

You need to download and install a plugin called Pretty Link Lite. Just search for it in the Plugins section of your Dashboard.

Once installed, you'll have a new section in your Dashboard for "Pretty Link".

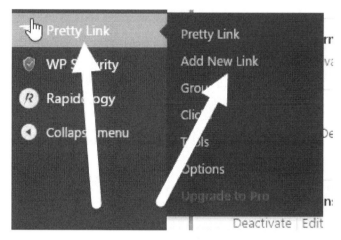

One of the menu items is **Add New Link**. Click it to set up a trackable link:

Add Link

Redirection* ⓘ	307 (Temporary) ▾
	Make your life easier by upgrading to Pretty Link Pro -- get more redirection results from your links by going pro today!
Target URL* ⓘ	https://www.amazon.com/s/ref=nb_sb_noss_1?url=search-alias%3Daps&
Pretty Link* ⓘ	http://▮▮▮.com/ wordpress2017
Title ⓘ	Wordpress 2017 on Amazon

Leave the **redirection type** at the default 307.

Copy and paste the URL to your Amazon book page in the **Target URL** box.

In the **Pretty Link** section, add a short identifier that will make up the URL. In this case, I added wordpress2017. It's best to add something short and meaningful to make it easier for you to remember and for people to type into their browser.

In the title box, add a short headline. If you leave this blank, the plugin will visit the page specified in the Target URL box, and use the page title from there.

When you are done, save your pretty link. This is the simple process you go through every time you set up a link you want to track.

All of the URLs you set up like this will appear in a list in the **Pretty Links** screen.

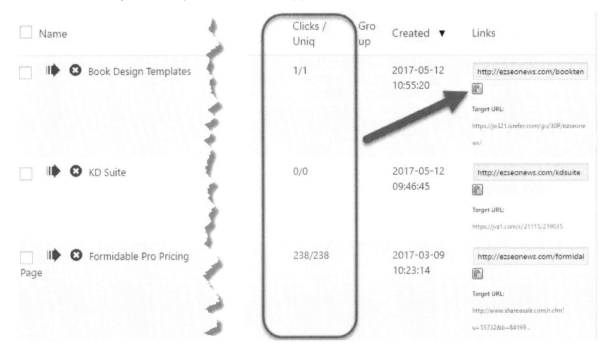

When you want to place a trackable link somewhere, you can grab it using the copy button under the link.

When a pretty link is used in the YouTube description, or embedded in an article on any website you submit content to, it will redirect the visitor to the Amazon product page for the book. On top of that, it will record the click data for that link.

You can quickly view your click data within the Pretty Link plugin screen. In the screenshot above, I've highlighted the clicks column. It contains two numbers.

The first of the two numbers represents the total number of clicks on that URL. The second number represents the unique number of clicks on that URL (how many people made those clicks).

See how valuable this can be?

To make use of this strategy to see where traffic is coming from, create a unique pretty link for each location you want to place a link.

Each of these links will point to the same product page on Amazon, but you'll be able to track how many times each link was clicked, telling you where the traffic to your Amazon book page came from.

YouTube is something you should probably experiment with, especially if you write non-fiction.

Tracking sales of your book

You can track sales (and free downloads), of your book by logging into KDP.

Across the top you'll see a menu:

Bookshelf | Reports | Community | KDP Select

Click on the Reports link.

Sales Dashboard	Historical	Month-to-Date	Payments	Pre-orders	Promotions	Prior Months' Royalties	Ad Campaigns

You have several options across the top of the reports screen.

Sales Dashboard – This screen shows real-time sales of your books. You have a lot of options available to you. For example, you can just look in one of the Amazon marketplaces at a time, or all of them combined. Similarly, you can look at sales of just one book, or all books combined. You can also specify the date range.

Data on the sales dashboard is displayed as both graphs and table. The table at the bottom will give you a quick indication of how much your royalties are going to be, though this table does not include Kindle Edition Normalized Pages (KENP) read. This is the total number of pages read from borrows of your book. KENP adds a little more to your royalty total.

Historical – This screen shows historical sales and the "KENP read" for your books. Again, you can look at individual books or marketplaces.

Month-to-date – This is a snapshot showing you how you are doing so far, this month. It's a table listing your books, units sold, units refunded, KENP read, etc.

Payments – This shows all payments made to you from each of the Amazon marketplaces.

Pre-Orders – Shows details of any pre-orders you may have setup.

Promotions – This screen lists the Kindle Countdown promotions you have made, with a summary table showing how many units you sold at each price increment.

Prior Months' Royalties – This screen shows you the royalties for every month you have been publishing. You can view these online in a table, or download the data as an excel spreadsheet.

Ad Campaigns – If you run any Amazon advertising campaigns, you will find details on this tab.

Other eBook platforms

This book deals with publishing on Amazon only. It is worth knowing that there are other platforms on which to publish your books. The thing is, we are using KDP Select on Amazon to offer our books on a 5-day free promo, and while the book is enrolled in KDP, you CANNOT publish it in any other digital format. The initial KDP enrollment lasts for 90 days.

Amazon has it set up so that your books will automatically be re-enrolled once a 90-day period is up, so if you want to cancel KDP enrolment, remember to go in and change the setting manually before the 90 period is up.

Once you are no longer enrolled in KDP Select, you are free to publish your books on any other platforms you like.

If publishing on other platforms is of interest to you, research Smashwords.

As a final note to this section, I do want to mention something about these other platforms. From talking to other writers, sales on these alternative platforms generally yield a much smaller percentage of sales when compared to Amazon (just 1 – 2% in many cases).

Things may change and other platforms may become more popular in the future, but remember, Amazon Kindle books are not just available on Kindle devices. They are available on PCs, Macs, Smartphones, iPhones and Android tablets. In other words, if someone wants to read your Kindle book, they can.

You can read my post if you want more details on this:

https://goo.gl/F74nyj

Non-US publishers

If you live in the US, then you can ignore this section.

If you live outside the US, then you MUST read this segment.

Firstly, let me add a disclaimer.

I am not a lawyer. The information included in this section is based on my own experience with the whole tax issue. You should not take anything I say as legal advice, it is for information only.

OK, let's get on with it.

The number one thing you need to know is that you DO have to declare your Kindle royalties in the country where you live. That means paying taxes where you live on any royalties Amazon sends you. That is **in addition** to what I describe below.

If you live outside the US, then there's another major inconvenience that you have to deal with.

Amazon will withhold 30% tax on all of your royalty earnings and send it to the US Internal Revenue Service (IRS).

It's a double whammy. First Amazon takes 30% off your royalties and sends you a check for the remainder. You then pay tax in your own country on whatever is left.

OK, so the good news...

If your country of residence has a tax treaty with the US, you can reduce this 30% withholding significantly, even down to zero in some cases. To do this, you need to fill out the tax forms on Amazon.

Contact Amazon if you need more information on this process.

Where to go from here

Hopefully, the first section of the book will have given you everything you need to know about publishing & promoting on Amazon Kindle. Your next step is, therefore, to finish your book and publish it.

If you want to go deeper into publishing on Kindle, and you are particularly interested in writing fiction books, then there is one course that I can highly recommend. It's by a successful Kindle author called Geoff Shaw (though you won't find his books on Amazon as he writes under pen names).

He does place a lot of emphasis on fiction writing, so if you are interested, you can read my review of his course here:

https://goo.gl/boJoDW

His program is the most complete course on Kindle Publishing that I've come across, and if you ever get stuck, he's super quick at replying to emails.

Create the paperback

I sell more paperbacks than Kindle editions of my books. That is common for non-fiction writers, less so for fiction writers. However, creating a paperback from your existing Kindle manuscript is easy, so why not? The next section of this book covers publishing on Createspace, Amazon's own, print-on-demand service.

Publishing as a Paperback

Createspace is a print-on-demand service owned by Amazon.

If you are creating Kindle books, it's relatively easy to convert those books into physical paperback versions, without having to pay anything up front. It works like this:

1. Create your book in Createspace format.

2. Submit it for publication.

3. When approved, promote your book.

4. Let Amazon & Createspace do the rest.

If you make a sale, Createspace prints a copy of your book, then packages and sends it to the customer. At this point, Createspace takes its cut and gives you your royalty.

As you can see, this is pretty much hands-off on your part. All you need to do is promote your book, but Amazon will also do that for you. You don't have to worry about taking orders, shipping, refunds, etc. All you do is collect your royalty payments every month.

This section of the book will take you through the complete process.

You've already created your Kindle book from your Word document and we'll now use the same Word document to create the paperback version. Most of the work has already been done. All we really need to do is decide on page size, create a cover, and then do some final checks of the document.

How big will your book be?

Your book is going to be printed on paper, but what size paper? And what margins do you need around the edges of that paper to make sure text isn't obscured by the spine of the book or cut off during final trimming?

The size of the book will impact how much of a royalty you make from each sale, so let's look at a price calculator to help you decide the size that gives you the biggest return.

Price calculator

Head on over to this page on Createspace (you do not need to be logged in):

https://www.createspace.com/Products/Book/

Click on the **Royalties** tab and scroll down to the calculator:

You need three important pieces of information before you can work out royalties:

1. Interior type (Black & White for us).

2. Trim size (still to be determined).

3. Number of pages (affected by trim size).

Obviously 2 & 3 above are dependent on each other. The larger the trim size, the more content per page, and the fewer pages.

In Word, on the **Page Layout** tab, click the **Size** button and you'll see what size you are currently using:

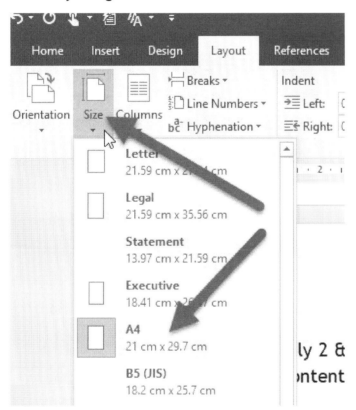

You can also see how many pages Word says the book contains:

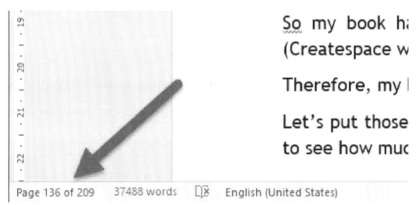

This book has 209 pages when it uses a trim size of 21 cm x 29.7 cm (my Word is using centimeters, Createspace works in inches, so to convert these into inches we divide by 2.54).

Therefore, my book has 209 pages at 8.27" x 11.69". That option is not available in the Amazon calculator:

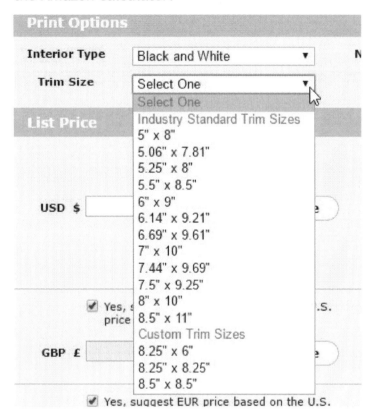

Therefore, the first thing I am going to do is change the page size of my document in Word to one that is available, and close to what I already have. Let's choose 8.5 x 11 inches.

I can find out those dimensions in centimeters by multiplying my 2.54.

Therefore, my book needs to be reformatted to 21.59 cm x 27.94 cm.

From the Layout tab, I can select that option from the **Size** button.

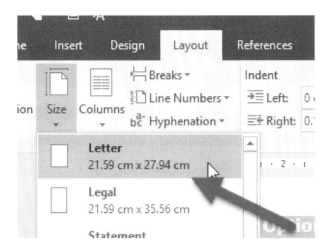

To make sure your whole document uses the same trim size, select the entire document before you change the trim size. On Windows computers, you can do that by pressing CTRL + A to select the whole book and then make your choice of trim size.

Word will reformat the book, meaning the number of pages is likely to change.

The book now has 241 pages.

Let's put these figures into the calculator with an initial price of $10, and press calculate:

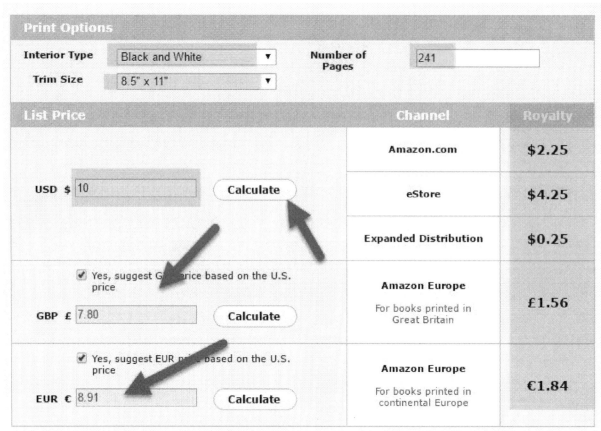

		Print Options		
Interior Type	Black and White ▼		Number of Pages	241
Trim Size	8.5" x 11" ▼			

List Price		Channel	Royalty
		Amazon.com	**$2.25**
USD $ 10 Calculate		eStore	**$4.25**
		Expanded Distribution	**$0.25**
☑ Yes, suggest G___ price based on the U.S. price GBP £ 7.80 Calculate		**Amazon Europe** For books printed in Great Britain	**£1.56**
☑ Yes, suggest EUR ___ based on the U.S. price EUR € 8.91 Calculate		**Amazon Europe** For books printed in continental Europe	**€1.84**

*Figures generated by this tool are for estimation purposes only. Your actual royalty will be calculated when you set

OK, so on Amazon.com, I'd make $2.25 per sale.

What if we changed the book format to something smaller?

Well, if I formatted my book to 6" x 9", which is a common size, my book would increase to 363 pages.

Let's plug that into the Createspace calculator with the same $10 price tag:

Amazon.com	$0.79
eStore	$2.79
Expanded Distribution	-$1.21
Amazon Europe For books printed in Great Britain	£0.34
Amazon Europe For books printed in continental Europe	€0.38

Because the book is a lot longer, it costs more to produce, therefore gives me less royalty per sale.

In this case, I'd make $0.79 per sale, instead of $2.25. I'd also make a loss on expanded distribution. Clearly, I could not afford to sell the book for $10 with this smaller trim size.

Have a play around with sizes for your books and see how trim size and book-length will affect the royalty you earn. For my book, I am choosing the largest standard format (8.5 x 11), to keep the number of pages to a minimum. You may not be able to do that if you are writing fiction books, as that would just look weird in many cases, but for non-fiction, with 100+ pages, it's fine.

Choose your trim size and set it in Word before continuing.

Converting to Createspace Format

We are going to check the Word document for a few common problems, but before we do, I just want to make sure we are all starting from the same place. You should already have your book written in Word, and have it published on Kindle.

After following the previous section of the book, your Word document should have:

1. A title page.

2. Disclaimer / Copyright information.

3. Table of Contents.

4. Page numbers.

5. All Word styles like Normal, Heading 1, Heading 2, etc. correctly used.

6. A good quality font, that you do have the license to use in a print book.

Make sure the above checkpoints are all true for your document before you move on.

Before we do anything, save a copy of your Word file as a separate Createspace/paperback version. That way, any changes you make (and they will be minor), will only affect the paperback version of your book.

Check #1 – Page Size & Margins

Make sure that your Word document is setup to use the correct page size and margins you chose earlier. You can find the settings for these on the **Layout** tab:

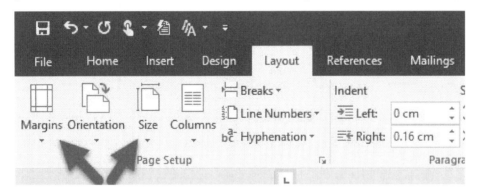

Check #2 – Correct use of styles

We need to make sure the styles we have used in our Word document are correct. They should be. After all, you have already published your book on the Kindle platform, and styles needed to be correct there. Nevertheless, go through your document and make sure that paragraphs use the "normal" style, main headings use "heading 1" and so on.

Check # 2 - Links

This check is a simple one too. If you have used hyperlinks in your book, make sure they are short enough for the reader to type into a web browser. Do not create hyperlinks like this, because paperbacks aren't clickable. Instead, if it is a short URL that is easy to write, like google.com, then write the full URL. Otherwise, use the Google URL shortener to present the URL in an easily copied format, e.g. https://goo.gl/boJoDW

Check #3 - Numbered Lists

Go through your book and make sure that bullets and numbered lists look OK. Also, make sure that numbered lists start from the right number. If you are making use of the built-in numbered lists in Word, beware. I have had a lot of problems with numbered lists not starting at 1. The list seems to think it is part of a previous list. You'll spot this in your book because your list won't start at number 1.

You can reset the starting number of any list in Word, but I got tired of this problem and do not use numbered lists anymore. If I want a numbered list, I will just type the list as normal text, e.g.

1. Raspberry sauce

2. blueberry sauce

3. Pancakes

That list does not use the built in numbered list format, and I've indented the list by simply using the tab key.

Whatever you choose, go through your book and make sure all numbered lists begin with the correct number.

Also make sure that if you use bullet lists, they look OK. Sometimes you can find bullet list items are formatted as child items and indented further than they should be. I also avoid the bullet feature in Word and just create them manually on my PC by holding the ALT key and typing 0149. That will create a • for you.

Check #4 - Layout

This is a simple check, but an important one. With the Kindle document, the spacing between lines was automatic and simple. The rule was never to use empty lines to space things out. With Kindle, you used the pre-formatted styles like "normal" and "Heading 1", to apply uniform spacing in the document.

The reason for that was the same reason we didn't want page numbers in the Kindle format – Kindles don't have "pages".

Physical books obviously do, so we need to check the layout for a few common problems.

Problem 1 – Empty lines at the top of a page

This should not happen if you have made sure you have no empty lines (remember the pilcrow?), but do go through and make extra sure. I always proof my books with two pages visible in Word. Therefore, this type of problem is easy to spot:

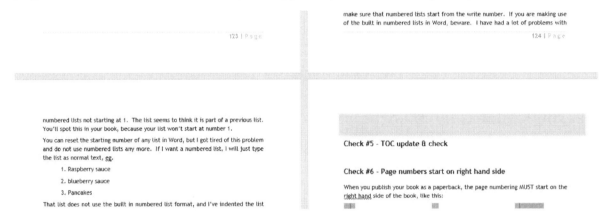

In that screenshot, can you see the gap at the top of the right-hand page?

That gap is essentially a misplaced pilcrow and needs to be removed. Go through your document and make sure there are no gaps at the top of pages.

Problem 2 – Headers at the bottom of pages

This problem isn't restricted to headers. It actually includes anything that appears at the bottom of the page but would be better off starting at the top of the next page. For example, here is a header that should be moved to the top of the next page:

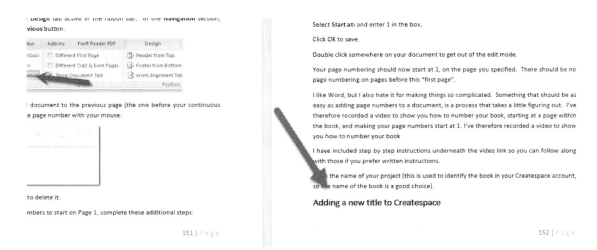

That headline is right at the bottom of the page and should be moved onto the next page. There are two ways to do this. Simply add in a line space (yes, a pilcrow), or insert a "new page" break so that the headline appears at the top of the next page. I recommend you use the page break option.

Can you think of other situations that might require a page break? What about this:

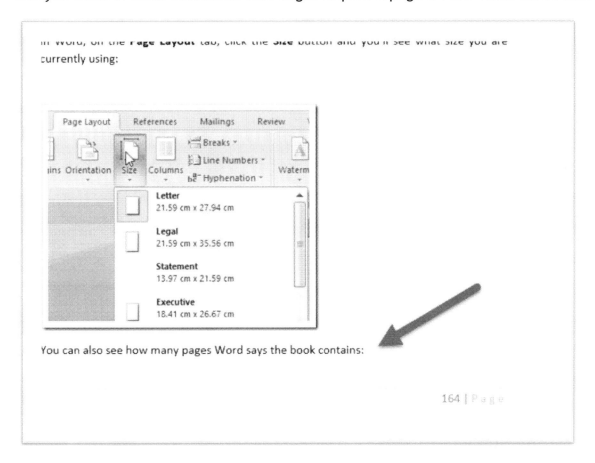

The page ends with a colon, and the image that the colon refers to is on the next page. It doesn't look great.

Colons like this are usually followed by something important, so it is best to keep it all on the same page. Add a page break to make sure the colon is on the same page as the information it refers to.

Check #5 - TOC update & check

The next step is to update your table of contents to make sure page numbers are correct. This should always be one of the final checks because if you need to go back in for editing, layout or page spacing, the page numbers can change for specific headlines and screw up the table of contents. Therefore, complete other checks first, then update the TOC.

Once updated, check to see if you want to edit the TOC further. For example, the pages that appear in your book BEFORE the first numbered page may appear in your TOC and need to be edited out of the TOC. Here is mine for this book:

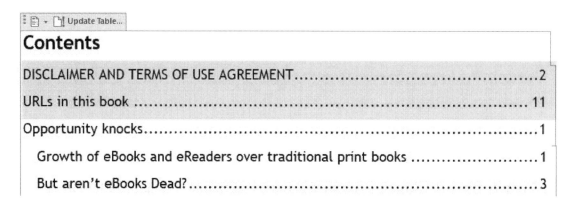

Those two lines need to be removed from the table of contents, and can simply be highlighted and deleted.

Check #6 - Page numbers start on right-hand side

When you publish your book as a paperback, the page numbering MUST start on the right-hand side of the book, like this:

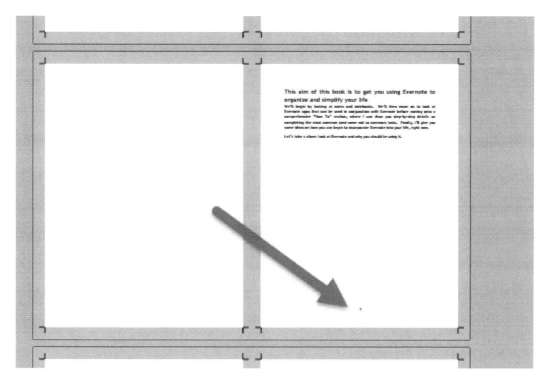

Failure to do so will mean your book will not be accepted by Createspace until you fix it.

Before this first numbered page, you have the title page, disclaimer, table of contents, and maybe some other stuff. It can, therefore, be a little confusing trying to make sure your first numbered page in on the right-hand side. The easiest way of checking this is to count your pages from the beginning. The first numbered page should be an "odd" page (1, 3, 5, 7, 9 and so on).

As I am writing this book, I just checked and my first numbered page is the 11th page, so I am fine. However, be aware that updating any page before this first numbered page, e.g. TOC, can change the number of pages at the start of the book, so this check should be completed after all others.

Check #7 – Image DPI "requirements"

When you take a screenshot, the software you use will probably be capturing at between 72 – 100 DPI. DPI is a measure of the number of "dots" that are used in an inch to create the image. When you publish a book on Createspace, they will tell you that you need 300 DPI images, and you do if you want every image crisp. However, that is not possible with screenshots, because although you can convert them to 300 DPI, you are converting from 72 DPI so the image won't be any clearer.

If you have the problem that images are lower than 300 DPI, and you cannot do anything about them, e.g. screenshots, then don't worry about it. You can still publish your book. Createspace calls this a "non-blocking" issue. In other words, the issue won't block the book from publication.

Images in Word

Word might compress images in your documents and reduces their DPI. To check, and to fix this issue, we first need to save the Word document using the Save As button.

In the dialog box that opens, click the Tools menu,

and select Compress Pictures.

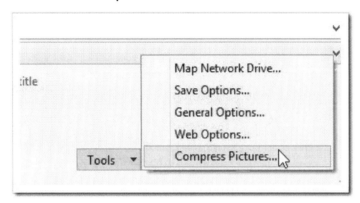

The Compress Pictures dialogue box opens up:

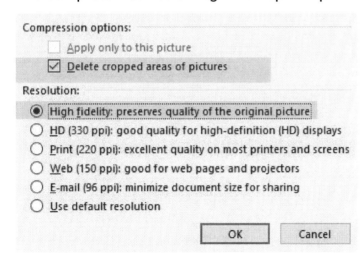

Select the box to delete cropped areas of pictures, and select **High fidelity** to make sure images are not compressed.

Click the OK button.

Now click the **Save** button to save your document.

What we have just done is turn off the compression of images *for this document only*. When you create your next book, remember to save your document this way the first time.

Adding a new title to Createspace

With the book finally ready, it's time to add the book to Createspace.

If you haven't already got an account on Createspace, then go and get one.

https://www.createspace.com/

Once it is all set up, log in.

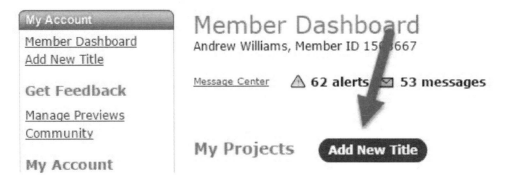

Click the button to **Add New Title.**

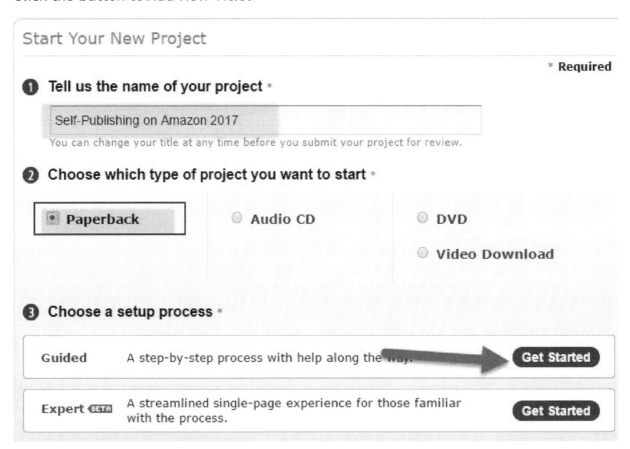

Fill in the name of your project (this is used to identify the book in your Createspace account, so the name of the book is a good choice).

Click the paperback option, and then click the **Get Started** button next to the Guided option.

Title Information   ◀ Back   Next ▶

What to do on this page: Enter title information, including title and author. This information is associated with your book's ISBN and cannot be changed after you complete the review process.

* **Required**

Title *	Self-Publishing on Amazon 2017
Subtitle What's this?	No publisher? No Agent? No Problem!

Primary Author *
What's this?

Dr	Andy		Williams	
Prefix	First Name / Initial	Middle Name / Initial	Last Name / Surname *	Suffix

Add Contributors
What's this?   Authored by   ▼   **Add**

☐ This book is part of a series (What's this?)

Series Title		**Volume**	▼

Edition number
What's this?   1.0

Language *
What's this?   English   ▼

Publication Date
What's this?

Save   **Save & Continue**

Fill in the title, subtitle, and the author name. You can add additional contributors, e.g. another author, editor, illustrator, etc., by selecting the type of contributor and clicking the **Add** button in the **Add Contributors** section.

You can also enter a series title and volume if applicable. If you used this when submitting your Kindle version, use the same series information for the paperback.

Enter an edition number and language but leave the publication date blank. Createspace will automatically fill this in for you when you submit your files for review.

Click **Save & Continue.**

You will now be asked if you want to provide an ISBN number yourself or use a Createspace one. I won't go into the differences here, but for my non-fiction books, I am using a Createspace assigned ISBN.

If you want to understand your choices, read this article:

https://goo.gl/Fs7NGw

Select the **Free Createspace-Assigned ISBN** and click the **Assign Free ISBN** button.

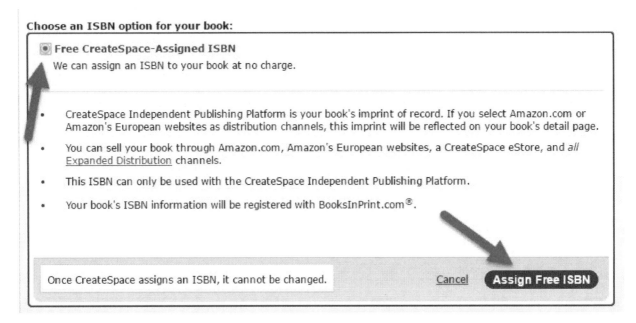

You will get a message saying that the ISBN is now locked and cannot be changed for your book.

Click **Continue** to proceed.

You now need to choose the paper and trim size for your book. Again, this can be changed later, so for now, just choose **Black & White interior**, **White paper** (though cream is nicer in fiction books I believe), and the trim size you chose earlier.

Further down the page, click on the **Upload your book file** radio button.

The screen expands with a new button to browse for your book. The instructions on this page suggest that you can upload the following formats: PDF, DOC, DOCX, and RTF. In fact, I have never had any luck uploading Word documents. It always generates an error:

Choose how you'd like to submit your interior:

Upload your Book File
You can upload your work as a print-ready .pdf, .doc, .docx, or .rtf. Your page count will be detect automated print check will run once your upload is complete. You'll be able to see any issues onl Interior Reviewer tool.

Interior File * [   ] **Browse**

The following formats are accepted: pdf,doc,docx,rtf

⊗ **We were unable to read your file. Try uploading your file as a .PDF.**

NOTE: I have successfully uploaded some DOCX files in the past, but found the layout was screwed up on some pages. Therefore, I recommend you save your book as a PDF and upload that instead. A page in the PDF document is an actual page in the book, so you can be sure your paperback will turn out fine.

To save your book as a PDF, simply go to File, Save As, and select PDF.

Upload the PDF to Createspace by selecting the PDF document and making sure the **Bleed** is set to **Ends before..:**

Bleed *
What's this?

Ends **after** the edge of the page ◯

Ends **before** th edge of the p ◉

Now click **Save**.

Once uploaded, Createspace does an automated **Print check** and will report back on any problems it finds.

My book has a lot of screenshot images and these will all generate errors because they are 72 dpi screenshots.

Here is my report:

UPLOAD RECEIVED!   Edit your Interior Details

self-publishing on Amazon 2017.pdf 242 pages,
8.5" x 11" (21.59 x 27.94 cm)
Black & White on White paper

⚠ Our automated print check found 4 issues with your file.

• Get more information on the issues we found.

• See useful guides that show your trim size and print
  margins where they matter: with your content.

• Check for typos, grammar, and formatting problems.

⚠ Your web browser does not currently support Flash Player 10.2, which is required to open Interior Reviewer. For
instructions on how to get Flash Player, go here.

Upload a different file   Launch Interior Reviewer   Skip Interior Reviewer

I have 4 issues!

Launch the Interior Reviewer to explore these issues. As you can see in the screenshot, the button is disabled in Google Chrome. You can fix this if you have the same issue. Please read this page for instructions:

https://goo.gl/v1BcQA

Once enabled, I can open the reviewer. When it opens, a pop-up will appear on top of the reviewer with a few instructions. Read them! Then click **Get Started.**

The issues are highlighted in the right-hand margin. The first problem is this:

> This PDF file was submitted at a size different from the expected trim size. We have attempted to place the content on the page in a reasonable location. Please check each page to make sure everything appears as expected. If the content is not aligned properly please resize your PDF to match the trim size and upload again.

That's a surprise. It's not an error I have seen before, and clearly, I have forgotten to check the trim size in Word.

To fix this error, make sure the Word trim is set to the same size as the one selected inside the Createspace, before saving the PDF. As mentioned earlier in the book, when you change the trim size of your document, you must select the whole document first, otherwise, your new trim size will only be applied to the section of the document you are currently in.

That's the problem in my case. I hadn't selected the whole document before changing the trim:

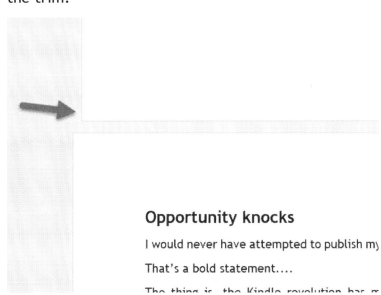

Opportunity knocks

I would never have attempted to publish m[y]

That's a bold statement....

The thing is, the Kindle revolution has m

"Opportunity knocks" is the first page that has a number and is in a different section from the page above it. I can see that the page before it is actually a different size. Therefore, to fix this, I need to change the page size again but select the whole document first (CTRL+A on Windows).

That will fix this error.

The next problem is an expected one:

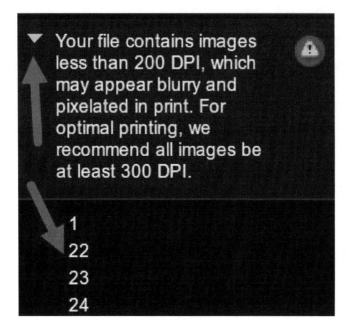

If you get this problem, you can click the little arrow top left and a drop-down list of all pages with this problem will appear underneath.

The thing is, while this is marked as a problem, you can ignore it. Your book will still be published. The only thing you should do is go through the reviewer and look at some of these images to see if they are going to be clear enough in the printed book.

Here is one that I have navigated to, and enlarged:

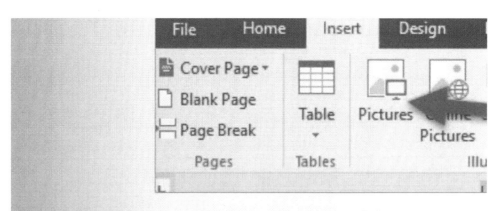

You'll be shown an image selection dialogue box, s insert button to insert it into your document.

It will be fine in the final printed book.

The next problem is this one:

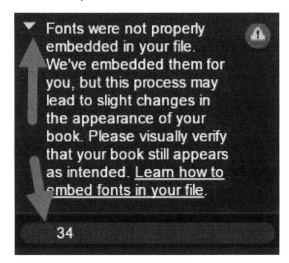

The problem appears on page 34. If I check it out, I can see that there is an issue with text formatting of the text:

For more details on book pricing and royalties, see these pages on mazon:

1. Pricing Page: https://goo.gl/t7e222
2. Sales & Royalties FAQ : https://goo.gl/FnJPtF

For now, your next step is to write your book. In the following section, we'll loc how you should format your book.

The "pricing page" and "Sales & royalties FAQ" text is gray. On closer inspection, it was text that had not been assigned the correct Word style, so was easy to fix. If you have a similar problem and cannot work out how to fix it, as long as the text looks OK in the reviewer, your book print will be fine, so don't sweat it.

The final problem I got was this one:

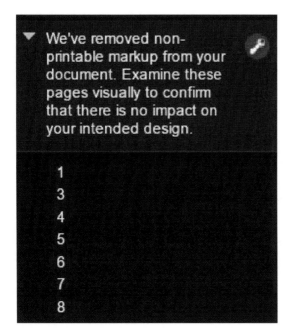

I am not totally sure what this means, but on inspection of those pages, it has something to do with my border/margins. However, again, this error will not cause you any problems if your book is displaying properly in the reviewer.

While we are in the reviewer, go to your first numbered page and make sure it is on the right-hand side:

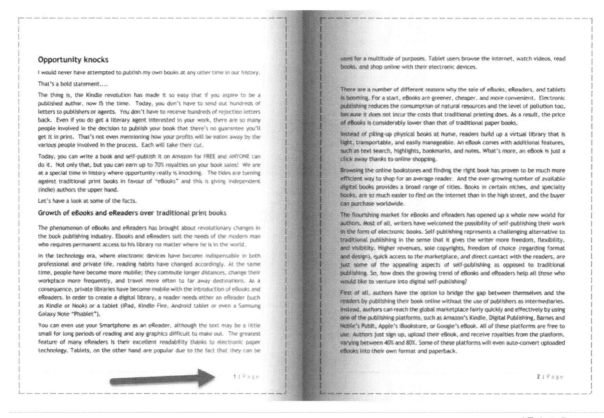

Whoops. Some changes I made to the book must have changed the number of pages at the start. Earlier when I checked, it was the 11th page, and therefore on the right. Now it must be an even page.

That's something that needs to be fixed. The easiest way is to insert a blank page (or delete one if you can) at some point BEFORE the first numbered page. Remember that the first numbered page should be an "odd" page. In my case above, it wasn't. It was the 12th page in the book and therefore appears on the left.

Another check you might like to do, and I always do this as a final check before approving the book, is to check page numbers in the book correspond correctly with the numbers in the table of contents. You don't need to check them all. Check a few at the start, middle, and end of the book, to make sure they are correct. If they aren't, this is easily fixed with an update to your TOC.

With the errors checked, I can go back into my Word document and fix things that need to be fixed. Once done, I'll resave as a PDF and upload again to check if the important errors have been fixed.

To get out of the reviewer, click the link at the bottom:

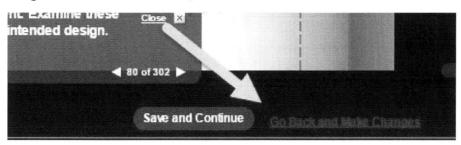

You can actually log out of Createspace now if you need a break. Everything we have done so far has automatically been saved.

Next time you log into Createspace, you can go back in and change settings, upload new versions of your book, etc., simply by clicking the link to the book (which is marked as incomplete until it is finally published):

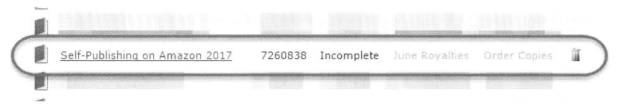

After you click on the title, select **Interior** from the options:

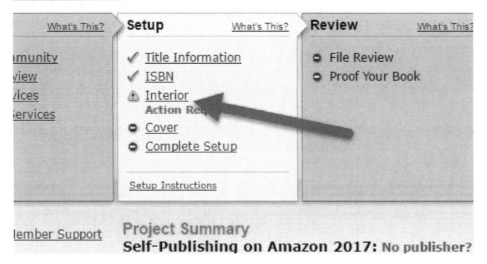

You'll be taken back to the Interior screen, showing errors, and allowing you to upload a different file:

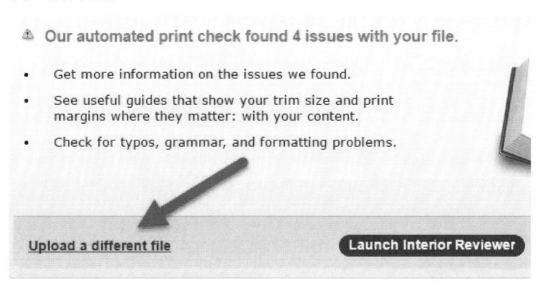

I made the changes to my own book and uploaded it again. It still had "problems", but the book looked fine in the reviewer, and therefore would print fine.

Once you are happy with your book, exit the reviewer, and click on the **Ignore Issues and Continue** button:

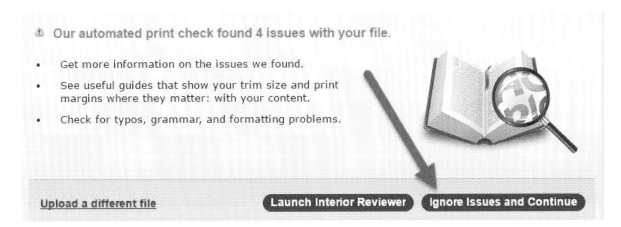

You will be taken to the Cover options page.

In the next section, we will look at how to create a cover image for your paperback book. Before you leave the reviewer, check how many pages your book has:

OK, so 223 pages of trim size 8.5 x 11.

Downloading a Cover Template

If you have the skills to design your own cover in Photoshop Elements or similar, then these instructions will give you the basics. If you believe that you cannot do this yourself, then you might be interested in using CreateSpace's online cover builder tool. You can access that on the Cover submission screen, so jump ahead to the chapter on submitting your cover if you want to check that out.

We know the trim size and we know the number of pages, let's go and grab a template we can use for the cover.

Createspace offers free cover templates for most trim sizes. You can find them here:

https://www.createspace.com/Help/Book/Artwork.do

When you get there, enter the details for your book:

.. and click the **Build Template** button.

You will then get a PNG template to download. The PNG file looks like this:

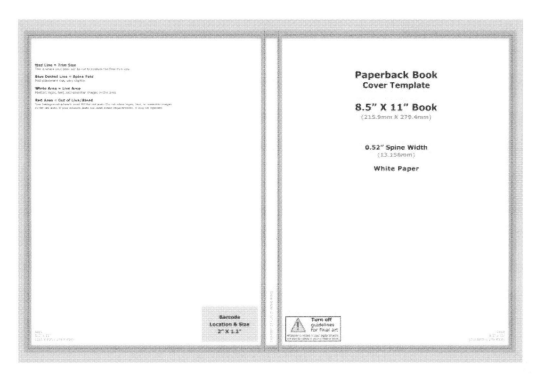

There are clear boundaries for where your cover content should and should not be. Keep content in the white areas.

Another source of cover templates can be found here:

http://bookow.com/resources.php

Scroll down the page a bit to get to the calculator. Fill out your trim size and page number. The script will then email you a template you can use.

Save the template somewhere safe on your computer.

Understanding the book cover templates

In the last chapter, we downloaded a template for our Createspace book cover.

Although it's beyond the scope of this book to show you how to create your cover, I will show you the basics

When you download a template, from either Createspace or the other site I told you about, you'll get a PDF file and a PNG file in the zipped-up download.

It's the PNG that we'll be using, so let's have a look at it.

You can load the PNG file into any image software, but one that works with layers is recommended. Adobe Photoshop Elements is ideal. Elements can also save the final book cover image as a high-quality PDF, which is the format we need for Createspace.

Areas marked on the templates

The areas marked on the template are very important, because they show you which parts will be used for the front, back, and spine of the cover. If we zoom into the template, we can see this border all around the template perimeter:

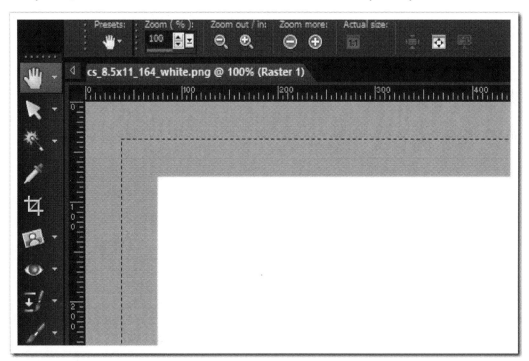

The white parts of the template show you which areas will be visible in the final cover, so make sure all important text, graphics etc., are contained within the white area.

The black dotted line is where the printers will be *trying* to cut the edges of the cover.

The red areas either side of this black dotted line are "bleed" areas. These areas MUST not contain anything essential to your final cover design, but they MUST be filled with part of your cover design. When the covers are cut, the cut may be a little to the left or right of the dotted line. By making sure the bleed area is not empty, the cover will look good even if the cut isn't exact.

Here is an example from one of my own covers:

You can see where the printer should be cutting the cover (dotted line emphasized with an arrow), but a little to the left, or a little to the right, won't make any difference to the final cover design.

The Spine

Depending on how many pages your book contains, you may be able to fit the title and your author name on the spine of the book. This is what the spine looks like in the template:

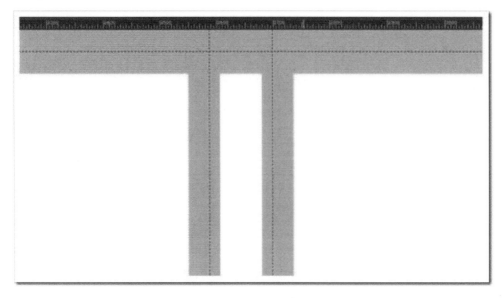

There are two parallel dotted lines running down the middle of the template. These mark the position of folds in the book cover that define the spine of the book. The white area in the middle is the printable area of the spine. Include title and author name inside here if you can. The spine has the red bleed areas as well because the fold in the cover may be a little to the right or left. Therefore, text in the spine must not touch the bleed area.

Here is the spine from one of my book covers:

ners 2017

Vordpress

er 250 screenshots).

'guru" in a few short hours, because
. Wordpress makes it possible for
nobbies, or business.

blute beginner, and get them building
ur hand, step-by-step, all the way.

start at the very beginning, and teach
Nordpress.

/ are reading about, so one thing this
em, showing you exactly what you will
s as you learn and master Wordpress.

(Spine text, vertical): Wordpress for Beginners 2017 - A Vi

Wordp
for Beginners.
Prepared www.boo
0.491" Sp e V
(12.47mm

You will notice that the spine text does not touch the bleed area. To the right of the spine, you can see part of the front cover design.

Here is the entire book cover, with elements positioned over the template:

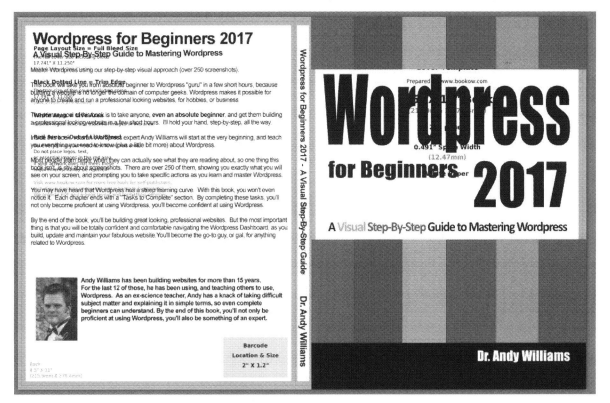

By adding a white background layer over the top of the PNG template, we get to see what the cover will look like on the book:

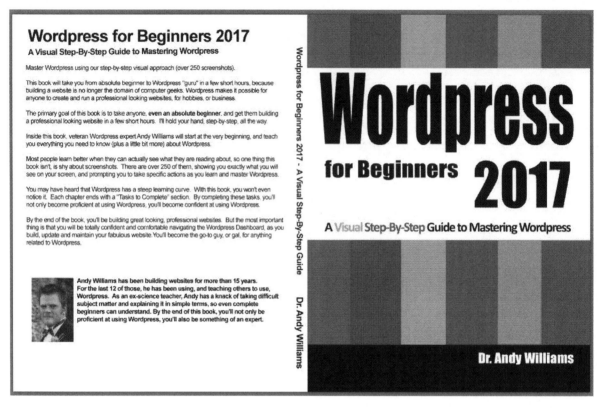

Obviously, you will need some skills to create your own cover, but you can still give it a go if you have Photoshop Elements or similar.

Once your cover is completed, you need to save it as a PDF. Create the PDF version of your cover in as high a quality as your software allows. The final PDF must be less than 40MB.

In Photoshop Elements, this is easy.

Go to File, Save As.

Select Photoshop PDF from the **Format** selector and click save.

A dialogue box opens up with some options:

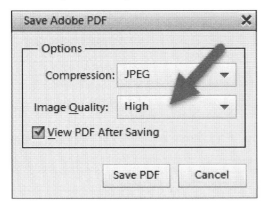

Make sure compression is set to JPEG and Image Quality is High.

Save your PDF cover.

Submitting the book cover to Createspace

In the previous chapter, we created the book cover. In this one, we need to submit it to Createspace.

First, log in:

https://www.createspace.com/

Now click the hyperlink to your book:

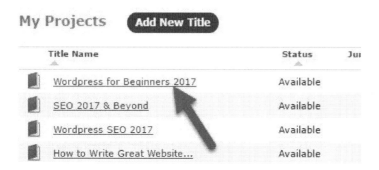

Now in the setup section, select **Cover**.

In step 1, you need to choose the finish on the book cover. You can choose from Matte or Glossy. For my non-fiction, I choose "glossy".

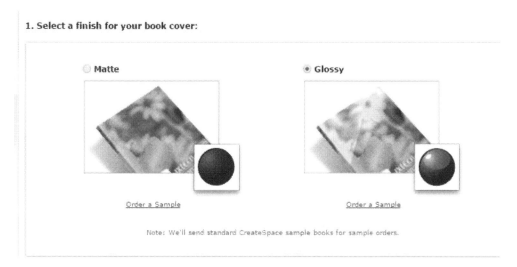

1. Select a finish for your book cover:

Matte

Glossy

Order a Sample

Order a Sample

Note: We'll send standard CreateSpace sample books for sample orders.

In step 2, you can choose from:

• Build Your Cover Online – Use CreateSpace's own cover builder to build your cover.

• Professional Cover Design – Hire someone from Createspace to build it for you.

• Upload a Print-Ready PDF Cover – which we did in the last chapter.

If you are insecure about your Photoshop skills, then the first option is worth looking at. Createspace provides this tool to help you create a cover. It's beyond the scope of this book to show you how to use that cover designer, but it is fairly intuitive.

If, like me, you created your own cover, then select **Upload a print-ready cover**, and upload your creation.

Once uploaded, you will see a **continue** button.

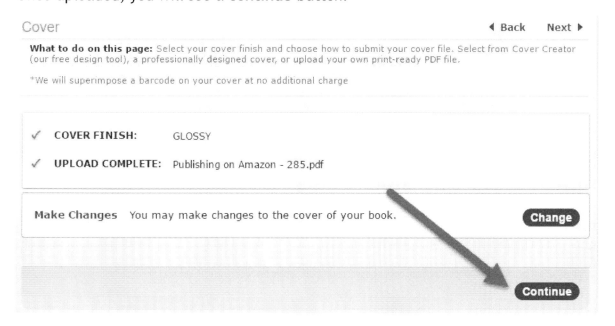

Cover   ◀ Back   Next ▶

What to do on this page: Select your cover finish and choose how to submit your cover file. Select from Cover Creator (our free design tool), a professionally designed cover, or upload your own print-ready PDF file.

*We will superimpose a barcode on your cover at no additional charge

✓ **COVER FINISH:**   GLOSSY

✓ **UPLOAD COMPLETE:** Publishing on Amazon - 285.pdf

Make Changes You may make changes to the cover of your book.   Change

Continue

You will be taken to a screen that summarizes your book submission:

The only thing you cannot edit at this stage is the ISBN.

However, if you are happy with your book and cover, and the internal reviewer looked fine, you can now click the **Submit Files for Review** button.

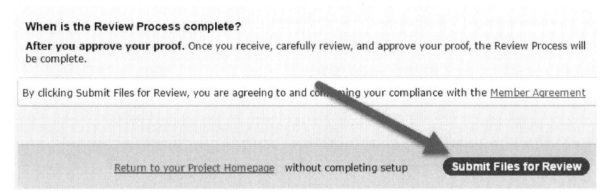

You will now see a dialogue box similar to this one:

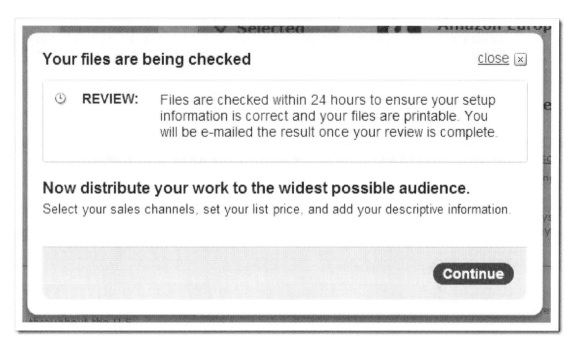

The files are going to be checked. That includes checks on the book and cover. They will check to make sure your book information has been entered properly. Title and author on the cover must match those details inside the book, and the details you submitted when adding your book to Createspace.

Within 24 hours, you should get an email with the results of their checks, and whether or not any further action is required on your part. If you've followed this book closely, your book should be accepted first time.

By default, your book will be available on Amazon.com, Amazon Europe stores, as well as the Createspace store.

While you wait, let's enter the pricing and distribution information.

Expanded Distribution?

Expanded distribution gives you a few more channels for book sales, and it is free.

I have mixed feelings about the expanded distribution options. The biggest problem is that an online seller can buy your books at a discount (Createspace offer your books cheaper through these channels as they are bulk purchases), and then sell them at lower prices than you do, effectively cutting off your sales. I actually do turn on **Libraries and Academic Institutions** for my books, but I recommend you do some more reading about these options before you enable any of them. You can come back later once your book is published and change your options here, so don't worry about selecting anything now.

Just **Save & Continue** to go to the book pricing page.

This is similar to the pricing calculator we looked at earlier in the book. However, now it's for real. We are choosing the real prices for our books.

Under each currency, you will be told the **minimum** price you can charge for the book. At that minimum price, you make zero in royalties:

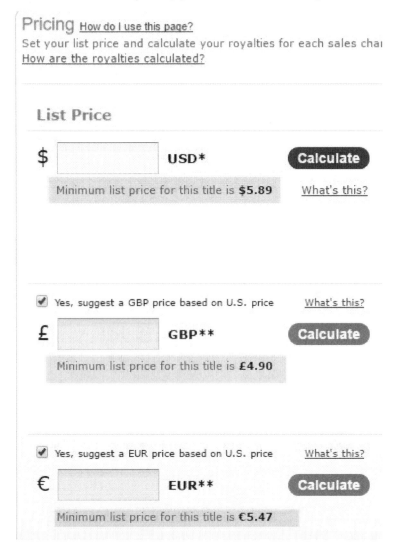

For my non-fiction, I like to start off at $9.99 and see where that takes me. Enter 9.99 in the USD box and click on **Calculate**.

List Price		Channel	Royalty
$ 9.99 USD*	Calculate	Amazon.com	$2.46
Minimum list price for this title is **$5.89** — What's this?		CreateSpace eStore	$4.46
		Expanded Distribution ⊖ Not selected - Select Channels	$0.46
☑ Yes, suggest a GBP price based on U.S. price — What's this?			
£ 7.81 GBP**	Calculate	Amazon Europe For books printed in Great Britain	£1.74
Minimum list price for this title is **£4.90**			
☑ Yes, suggest a EUR price based on U.S. price — What's this?			
€ 8.91 EUR**	Calculate	Amazon Europe For books printed in continental Europe	€2.06
Minimum list price for this title is **€5.47**			

There are checkboxes to automatically allocate prices in British pounds and euros if you want to use that feature. I tend to round up the suggested equivalent to x.99, so the suggested £7.81 would become £7.99 and the euro price would be rounded from €8.91 to €8.99.

When you make changes to the prices, click the **Calculate** button to check on the new royalty payment.

NOTE: You can change prices later (even once the book is published), so don't get too worried about this now.

Here are my final prices:

List Price		Channel	Royalty
$ `12.99` USD* **Calculate** Minimum list price for this title is **$5.89** What's this?		**Amazon.com**	**$4.26**
		CreateSpace eStore	**$6.86**
		Expanded Distribution ⊖ Not selected - Select Channels	$1.66
☐ Yes, suggest a GBP price based on U.S. price What's this? **£** `9.99` GBP** **Calculate** Minimum list price for this title is **£4.90**		**Amazon Europe** For books printed in Great Britain	**£3.05**
☐ Yes, suggest a EUR price based on U.S. price What's this? **€** `11.99` EUR** **Calculate** Minimum list price for this title is **€5.47**		**Amazon Europe** For books printed in continental Europe	**€3.91**

For a book sold via Amazon.com, I'd make $4.26 (compared to $1.37 for the Kindle version costing $2.99).

For a book sold at amazon.co.uk, I'd make £3.05 and in Europe, €3.91.

Once you have decided on your prices, **Save & Continue**.

After pricing, you'll be asked again to confirm the "cover finish", so select that and **Save & Continue** to the **Description** page.

You will need to enter a book description and choose a category for your book. Use the same details as the Kindle version.

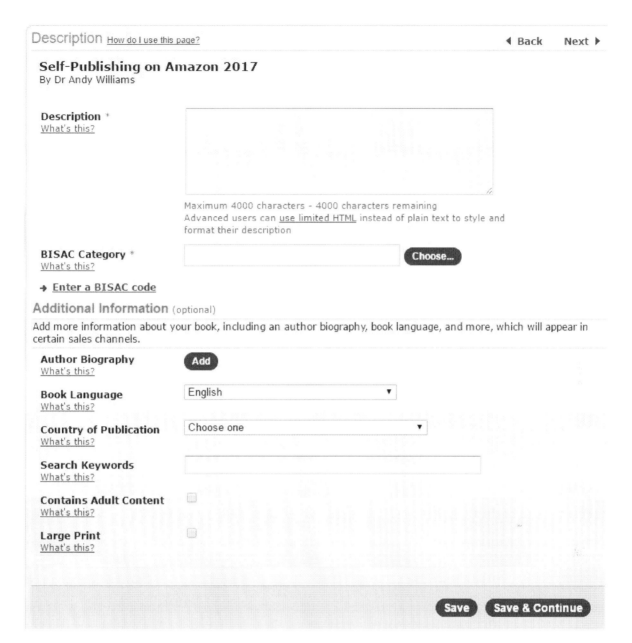

You can do basic formatting in the description by using some HTML, but do be careful and check what HTML is allowed. I personally stick to the bare minimum, usually just using it for bolding text. In the Appendix at the end of this book, I cover some basic HTML to help you.

Under Country of Publication, if you are using a Createspace assigned ISBN, you must set this to the United States.

Add some relevant search keywords (again, choose the same words as the Kindle version of your book.

If your book contains adult content, check that box.

If your book has large print, check that one.

Click **Save & Continue**.

You'll be taken to a page asking if you want to Publish on Kindle. We've already done that so there is nothing to do here.

Now we need to wait for the review process to complete, and the email notification telling us what to do next ;)

Feedback from Createspace, and the next step

OK, your book has either been accepted as is, or you may have some work still to do. This chapter shows what we need to do once we hear back from Createspace.

I've had my email back from Createspace:

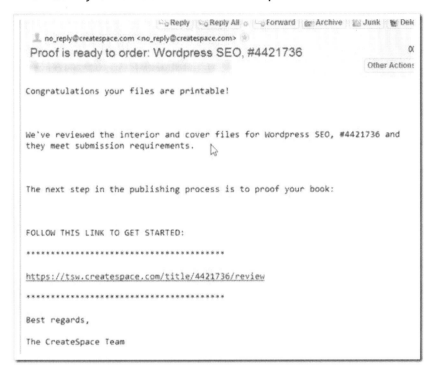

Everything is fine and I can proceed to the next step.

I was expecting an error or two called "non-blocking errors". Here's one I received earlier:

```
Our reviewers did find some non-blocking issues with your files.
Some of these issues may have been fixed causing alterations to your
files.

The interior contains images that are less than 200 DPI which may
appear blurry or pixelated when printed. For more information on
image resolution, please visit:
https://www.createspace.com/Help/Index.jsp?orgId=00D300000001Sh9&
id=50170000000Irmr
```

In this case, some of the images were less than 200 DPI. As long as you check the proofs, and zoom in to check images are legible, then this "less than 200 DPI" problem is not a major issue.

Why are these called non-blocking issues?

I think what they mean by non-blocking is simply an error that does not stop (or "block") the approval & printing process.

There is a link in the email to take you to the next step. When you click it, you are taken here:

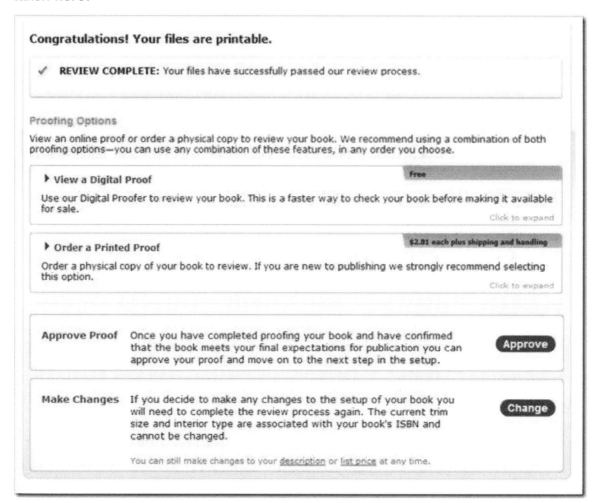

You need to do a final check before approving the proof for printing. Make sure your cover page looks as intended, and do proofread the content on the cover. I have had a book accepted in the past, but the digital proof showed problems with the cover – misaligned stuff or the spine folds not looking too good. Therefore, even though they accept your book and cover, do check it properly as well.

Go through the book one more time using the same checks we made earlier for layout, page numbering, and TOC.

Proofing the book again is very important. For the first few times, I actually recommend you order a printed "proof copy". Createspace provides these for the price of printing (and postage) only, so you are not paying full price for them. The only downside is the time these physical proofs can take to arrive, especially if you are outside the US.

Once you get used to Createspace publishing, you can just use the digital proof for problems.

Once happy, click the **Approve** button. Your book will then be made available on Amazon.

Once your book is available on Amazon, contact Createspace and ask them to link the paperback to the Kindle version.

Tell them the Createspace ID for the book:

.. and also the ASIN for the Kindle version:

This will mean that both versions are accessible from the same sales page:

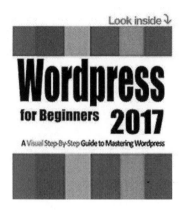

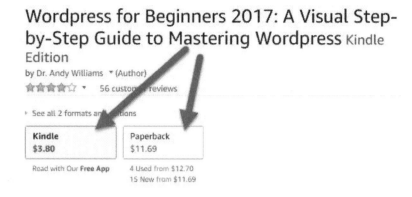

Any Kindle or paperback reviews you get will also be combined onto the same sales page.

This should be done automatically, but for me, it never is. Createspace will email you back telling you they have linked them, and in a few days, you should see Kindle and Paperback options within the Amazon marketplace.

Congratulations, you are now a published author!

Please leave a review/thought on Amazon

If you enjoyed this book, or even if you didn't, I'd love to hear your comments about it. You can leave your thoughts on the Amazon website.

Useful resources

There are a few places that I would recommend you visit for more information.

Publishing Tutorials

When I released the first version of this book back in 2013, I setup a web page to hold video tutorials. That page is here:

http://ezseonews.com/cspublish

It is a little dated now, but you might find some interesting tutorials there to help with your publishing efforts.

My ezSEONews Website

http://ezSEONews.com – This is my site where I offer free help and advice to webmasters. While you are there, sign up for my free weekly newsletter. You can also look through past issues and read articles on a variety of topics related to building WordPress sites.

My other Webmaster books

All of my books are available as Kindle books and paperbacks. You can view them all here:

http://amazon.com/author/drandrewwilliams

I'll leave you to explore those if you are interested. You'll find books on various aspects of being a webmaster such as creating high-quality content, SEO, CSS etc.

My Video Courses

I have a growing number of video courses hosted on Udemy. You can view a complete list of these at my site:

http://ezseonews.com/udemy

There are courses on the same kinds of topics that my books cover, so SEO, Content Creation, Wordpress, Website Analytics, etc.

Appendix I

HTML coding

For those who are interested, I want to show you how you can make your Kindle book descriptions a little less "ordinary" using formatting options that Amazon don't tell you about.

When you publish your book on Amazon Kindle, part of the process involves writing a book description so that Amazon can use that description on your book's product page. Amazon doesn't give you any formatting tools to make your descriptions more attractive, they accept plain text only. Here is an example of a plain book description:

Book Description
Publication Date: **June 21, 2011**

Reviews:

"Are there 'really' super foods and can we actually 'feel younger' when we eat them? Yes and YES!! I've been a leading expert in the nutrition and fitness industries since 1986 and I can tell you that this book is on to it. Use this info for just a few short days and you will begin to experience an energy and vitality you remember from years ago. Keep eating these foods and experience what it feels like to anti-age!!" - Donna Krech, Founder, ThinAndHealthy.com

Description:

From Almonds to Yogurt and Quinoa in between, here are 101 of the very best foods you can eat in order to live longer and look younger.

Discover these incredible superfoods:

" The common spice, available in any grocery store, that has antibacterial and antiviral properties and has more antioxidants than any other herb!

" The zero-calorie beverage that actually increases your metabolism and appears to fight against both cancer and aging.

" The gluten-free alternative to wheat that is loaded with protein, amino acids, and antioxidants.

" The "fun" fruit that has a powerful anti-inflammatory effect on the body and can lower the risk of heart disease and diabetes.

And 97 more!

You'll likely meet some new friends on this list along with foods that may already be a part of your diet. But they all share at least one thing in common: superfoods are foods that can have a profound impact on your health, vitality, well-being and even your longevity.

Lots of plain, boring text!

However, you also come across book descriptions like this one:

Book Description

Publication Date: **February 24, 2012**

Need Amazing Juicing Recipes? It's Time To "Juice Up Your Life:"

Drew Canole, the Star of Fitlife.TV and creator of the "Alpha Reset" Program is leading a movement around the country with his passion for helping people realize the healing and health-promoting powers of live, pure, fruit and vegetable juice.

Harnessing the power of live juices was the key to overcoming his own health issues and transforming his body to peak levels. **He has helped over 100,000 people** do the same and he shares his recipes and success strategies in this book.

Here Are 103 Delicious Juicing Recipes

...for healthy and satisfying fruit and vegetable juices! This is a newly updated version of Drew Canole's essential book to juicing and transforming your body.

Every juice recipe has been made, tested and selected to give you a diverse range of juices for taste, health, vitality, healing and longevity.

Rookies And Regular Juicers Both Love It Because...

It can be **confusing when you're first starting** out on your juicing journey what juices to make, how to make them and what health benefits you'll get from each. Drew lays out an easy to follow plan.

As a avid juicer, you might find yourself **bored of making the same juice**. Drew will show you how to spice it up and keep it fresh, ensuring that you'll keep juicing and enjoying the amazing benefits it brings your body.

.. and this one even has proper bullet points:

This Juicing Recipes Book You will Get

- Fruits and Vegetable Juicing Diet Plan Recipes for Weight Loss

- Detox and Cleanse Juice Recipes for Detoxification

- Juice Diet Recipes for Diabetes

- Juicing Recipes for Various Types of Cancer (Breast Cancer, Prostate Cancer, Lung Cancer)

- 100 of Juicing Recipes for Various Healthy Condition

- Breakfast Juice Recipes

- Juice Fast Recipes

- Health Benefit and Juicing Recipes for Beets

On the other hand, if you have always thought that the term "fasting" means skipping meals, this e-book will change your perspectives. As you go through an exploratory mission in this e-book, you will discover that **juice fast** is a fun way to lose weight by simply consuming delicious, refreshing, and pure juice and vegetable drinks. To make the **juice fast diet plan** a successful one, you will also be guided on how to make an ideal and **healthy juicing fasting plan**, **juicing diet plan** and **juice detox diet plan**. With the right plan, **juice fasting for weight loss** will be whole lot of fun.

So how are these authors adding text formatting to their documents?

Answer: Amazon allows standard HTML formatting, so let's look at that.

If you know some HTML, then you have a distinct advantage. If you don't, then it is quite easy. The main HTML tags you can use are:

<b>Bold</b>

So, if you want to make some text in your description bold, you surround that text with the <b></b> bold tag. The same goes for the following HTML tags:

<u>Underline</u>

<i>Italics</i>

<p>Paragraph</p> These tags space out paragraphs and can be used instead of using the <br> tag listed below. They do tend to leave large spaces between paragraphs, so do check this out when your description has been updated. I actually prefer to use the <br> tag instead.

<h1>H1 Header</h1> This is the largest of all headers and should appear only once at the top of your description. You can leave out the H1 altogether if you find it too big and just go with H2 as the main header.

Also <h2> to <h6>

There are a couple of useful HTML tags that don't "surround" other text. These are used as single tags where you want to insert that effect.

 Inserts a new line

<hr> inserts a horizontal line.

You can also use lists, like numbered lists or bullet lists. The HTML for these are a little more complex.

A numbered list:

<ol>

  <li>Item 1</li>

  <li>Item 2</li>

  <li>Item 3</li>

</ol>

A bullet list:

```
<ul>

  <li>Item 1</li>

  <li>Item 2</li>

  <li>Item 3</li>

</ul>
```

The only difference between a numbered list code and the bullet list code is the opening and closing tags to define the list. A numbered list is an "ordered list" so the list items are surrounded by <ol> </ol>. A bullet list is an unordered list so is surrounded by <ul> </ul>. Each list item in both types of list are enclosed in list item tags <li> </li>

The problem I find with lists like this is that the items in the list are spaced out too much. Therefore, I prefer adding bullets manually using the ALT + 0149 trick we looked at earlier in the book.

A Note on HTML formatting

A web browser starts to format text when it sees an opening HTML tag. The web browser knows when to stop applying that formatting because it encounters the corresponding closing HTML tag. If it does not find the corresponding closing HTML tag, it will continue formatting.

For example, if you add formatting but find the lower half of your description is all formatted as a headline, you've forgotten to close the headline tag.

Let's finish with an example of correct HTML formatting.

To create something in bold, there is an opening bold tag and a closing bold tag which wraps around the text you want bolded:

This is bold

Notice that the closing HTML tag includes a "/" before the formatting command. This symbol is the "stop" command in HTML. In this case, it means "stop bolding text here".

Therefore, when you add formatting to your book description, remember to add both the opening and closing HTML tags.

Printed in Great Britain
by Amazon